Advance Praise for

# *Surviving Online Dating Fraud*

Carole K. Zingula has accomplished here what so many people say they're going to do—write a book about something important in their lives. She's done a heck of a job unpeeling the many layers of an extremely painful chapter in her life. Kudos!

—Paul Rubin, Investigator

This book is a definite page turner. I found it hard to put down. It's utterly amazing what Carole K. Zingula went through with such grace, kindness, and strength. Two words for *Surviving Online Dating Fraud*: unbelievably awesome!

—Cheryl Rowley, Social Media Coordinator

In a powerful way, Carole K. Zingula brings to light the emotional pain and embarrassment of being scammed online. Her journey will bring hope and healing to others who have suffered through being taken advantage of by an online predator. Carole's perseverance and continued joy in life are an inspiration to all who know her.

—Steven D. Keist P.C., Attorney

*Surviving-Online Dating Fraud* reads like a historical novel—hard to lay down. I found Carole's writing style captivating and informative about a topic few people caught in the web of unscrupulous predators are willing to talk about. Her personal story of a humble beginning, dealing with marriage challenges, rising to the heights of her industry, searching for companionship, being scammed out of a small fortune, and now sharing the lessons she learned in this compelling book is astonishing.

—Lindsay A. Brady, Certified Hypnotherapist

After reading *Surviving Online Dating Fraud*, I was amazed at the depth and passion Carole K. Zingula reveals about her personal feelings regarding her family and the loss she experienced. She bares her soul to protect and help those who have already fallen into the hands of predators, wanting to assist other people from making the same mistakes.

—Roger Olewinski, IBM Branch Manager

Carole K. Zingula sets the stage in her book by sharing her youth and adult life with readers. The details of the crime against her are riveting and only surpassed by Carole's ability to pull herself up by her bootstraps and hold her head high. The real revelation in this book is Carole's courage throughout the ordeal, which has been displayed frequently in her passion to keep fit physically and mentally in the gym.

—Phil Eaton, Personal Trainer

During years hiding behind the shame, humiliation, and heartbreak of being a victim of fraud, I saw how dancing would ease Carole's pain and make her smile. Her writing in *Surviving Online Dating Fraud* reveals her caring heart, strong work ethic, physical stamina, and her determination to climb the mountain to success. She truly has shared her soul to help others.

—Mychael James, Professional Dancer/Instructor,
Franchisee Arthur Murray Studios

Carole K. Zingula's book invites us to see the inner workings of a human soul confronting the past by how her life unfolds in her future. This is no mere reporting of a horrific event, but a story that offers all of us an insight into why things happen in our lives and how we may influence the outcomes. Carole's brutal honesty and self-reflection reminds us that we are vulnerable to not only make mistakes, but that we have the ability to heal and recover. Life is not just a set of circumstances that we have to endure, but within it's strange and wondrous logic, life demands that we must learn from it.

—Apollo Spiritual Life Coach and Counselor

# Surviving
## Online Dating
## Fraud

**AUCTOREM**
HOUSE

# Surviving

## Online Dating Fraud

○ ○ ○

How I Recovered and
the Lessons I Learned

Carole K. Zingula

Auctorem House
276 5th Ave, Ste 704-2591
New York, NY 10001
www.auctoremhouse.com
Phone: 1 888-332-7718

Published by Auctorem House: 01/02/2025

ISBN: 978-1-965687-30-7(sc)
ISBN: 978-1-965687-31-4(e)

Library of Congress Control Number: 2024922855

# Contents

## PART III: CONVICTION, RESTITUTION, AND RECOVERY

## PART IV: HOW TO PROTECT YOURSELF

Dedicated to my children, Doug, Anna, and Susan.

They have shown me endless, unconditional love through this dark journey into recovery.

# Introduction

The FBI's Internet Crime Complaint Center (IC3), which provides the public with a means of reporting internet-facilitated crimes, reports that when compared to other online crimes, romance scams result in the highest amount of financial losses to victims. In their most recent available report of 2016, almost 15,000 romance scam complaints were reported—nearly 2,500 more than the previous year. In just one year, victims of online dating fraud lost $230 million.[1]

In 2012, at the age of seventy-six, I became one of those victims. In the story you're about to read, I will take you on my journey and tell you how and why I became one of ten people scammed out of thousands of dollars, all of us during the same time period by the same ring of criminals. Of these crime victims, I was the person defrauded out of the most amount of money: $400,000. Now, seven years later, I want to help you avoid being trapped by scam artists for any amount of money.

My case initiated the investigation of one of the largest online dating scams ever. At eighty-two years of age, I have recovered fairly well from the massive loss of my home and my income. After a great deal of personal work, I have elevated my self-esteem and recovered from the shame that comes from being duped out of hundreds of thousands of dollars. I now know my self-worth. Having traveled through six years of recovery, I want to share my journey with you. Being able to tell my story has led to new beginnings for me, including a newfound freedom to speak to others about this experience so that no one else has to suffer such an awful loss. After sharing my story, which will partly explain how scam artists were able to take advantage of me, I will teach you how you can protect yourself from online dating fraud—and other fraud as well. I will also list my recovery resources that may help you, if you, too, have been victimized by a con artist.

For years after these criminals stole from me, I searched for why this happened to me and how I might be to blame. Why would I or anyone be drawn into such a tragic and disillusioning trap? I believe there is a reason for all things, so from the beginning, despite my anguish, I asked myself what life lesson did I have to learn from this difficult experience? Embarking on this search for my WHY—all while feeling pain, happiness, fulfillment, and God's love—I found out the truth for myself: there *is* a reason for all things. My family history, my journey in life (the detours and specific paths I had taken) all led me to actions that help explain what happened to me and why.

Although the WHY is complex, the particular nature of my WHY became clear to me when I dissected the chapters of my life. We all make decisions every day, from childhood to death. We also all experience tragedies from which we learn life's lessons. This is my story and my lesson. I'm sharing it in hopes that the trauma and victimization that I experienced will help protect others from similar fraud. I also hope it will bring comfort to others who have been victims, so that they know they are not alone. There has been a new beginning for me. There can be a new beginning for you, too.

# Part 1

Family, Personal,
and Professional
History

# Childhood

He walked into the field, away from the house with the brown tattered suitcase in his hand once again. Why did I love him and dislike him at the same time? I loved him because he was my father, and he showered love on me for my birthday and special occasions. The aroma of roasted turkey and sage dressing coming from our simple 1940s kitchen still flood my mind and heart with fond memories. He was the master of homemade dressing and perfectly roasted turkey. It was a treat to our family of meager means. I disliked him because of the anger I felt when he said, "I'll be here tonight to help feed the chickens, pigs, and cows. We'll have ice cream before bedtime." But he didn't come home until way after bedtime. My mother, brother, and I did the chores and ate ice cream alone.

Often, I was still awake in my bedroom and could smell the alcohol when he came in the house. I could hear my mother asking him, "Why do you stay away at the tavern? You have a family here." Then I would hear a slap to her face and him say, "I work hard at my job. Is that not enough? I have work here, too, and never enough money for all of you. All I have ever known is work. Having a drink or two is my fun. If you don't like it, you can leave." It was always the same conversation.

I lacked respect for him. Summed up very simply, he drank too much alcohol, mistreated my mother, and was abusive to my brother and me. Each time he left with the brown tattered suitcase, I wished he would not return. But the pattern was always the same. He was gone a few days, and then his slim figure would appear across the field at sunset, as he made his way slowly to the house once again, only for the cycle to be repeated.

My brother and I did not feel unconditional love from my father. I was five years old, my brother seven, and the workload for us was heavy at a young age. Losing myself in a book, creative drawing, or dressing my dolls was wasted time even at a young age, in the eyes of my father. We were shamed for sitting down to read a book instead of working, and therefore we were assigned more chores.

My father was born and raised on a farm. When he was in eighth grade, he stopped going to school, due to the tragic loss of his mother. She had been killed by a bull in their barnyard, and my father was forced to leave his education behind and work with his father on the farm. He did a man's work at a young age. Was he transferring his own disappointment to my brother and I, unknowingly punishing us for what he couldn't have? Through the decades, I gained insight into perhaps what led him to his actions in those parenting years.

Our small, sparsely furnished country home was located on a seven-acre triangle of field and pasture along a two-lane paved country highway. As there was only a meager income from poultry and grain, my parents worked in town to supplement income. At ages five and seven, we were too young to stay alone for the summer.

Every spring, the Greyhound bus driver, with special instructions, stopped in front of our house on a designated day and hour. My brother and I stood in our gravel driveway, a small suitcase in each of our young hands, waiting eagerly for the big bus. As this big silver-and-gray bus approached, we yelled with excitement, our hearts pounding with joy at what was ahead of us for the summer. As the bus parked at the side of the highway, the driver, in his blue uniform and hat, called out to us, "Stay there, my little ones. I will walk you across." He made his way across the highway to our driveway, took each of us by hand, and as though we were his little loved ones, he took us safely across the highway. Boarding this gigantic bus, our legs were hardly long enough to reach the steps. But filled with excitement, we bounded up like rabbits, and took our seats to ride the sixty miles to our maternal grandparents for the summer.

Love and nurturance were abundant in my grandparents' farm home. I wanted to stay forever. My grandfather nicknamed me "Topsy" because he said, "You are tops in all you do." He always seemed pleased that I followed him around to learn everything I could. After I begged many times, he taught me how to milk the cows, but always with a reminder not to waste too much milk by squirting at the cats. I loved taking cold ginger water in the Karo Syrup can to him as he plowed the field with horses. The smell of the black soil being turned and the sweating horses still lingers with me. It didn't matter what I was doing. My grandfather always smiled and had an old-time story to share with me every evening.

My favorite stories were about the fire wagon and the team of neighbors who responded to the country fires. It was scary to hear him tell about the barn fires, but I loved to hear about the team working together to help contain fires and rescue animals. And, I always wanted to go with him when I heard the huge bell clanging, as the wagon came up the dirt road by my grandparent's farm.

A fire truck in Iowa farm country is different than what we think of as a fire truck today. A group of farmers had gotten together to organize a simple water wagon that would make some attempt at putting out barn fires, with a ray of hope to save animals and hay. It was a horse-drawn wagon with a large water tank mounted to it. A fire hose was then attached. It had no pressure, just simply a hose to fill buckets with water.—certainly, a very meager means of extinguishing a fire, small or large. Fifteen to twenty dedicated farmers would form a bucket brigade to try and keep a fire from getting totally out of hand. Many of the fires were started by lightning or combustion of the hay.

Finally, one night, most of the barn fires being at night, I heard the bell from the distant corner. We called this corner, "The County Line." Everyone, as usual, was hollering, "Fire, fire, fire, get up!" You could hear them coming closer and closer. Oh, I wanted to go with Grandpa so bad. He always said, "It's too dangerous, Tops. You need to stay with Grandma." He usually took the Model T when he heard them coming. I really didn't want to go in Grandpa's Ford to the site. I wanted to go with the wagon, hearing and feeling the pounding of the horse hooves. The driver could snap the whip ever so sharp to keep them moving. The excitement of alerting neighbors along the way would also be exciting. I begged once more, "Please, Grandpa, let me ride on the wagon. Just this once. Please, Grandpa, Please." Finally, after much begging, he lifted me up on the wagon, giving me stern instructions, "Don't move, sit there until they arrive, and, George, you look after her! I will hurry along in the Ford and meet you there."

The fire was about a mile from my grandparents' house. The sky was lit with orange and clouds of gray smoke. It was a hay fire. Everyone was yelling, "Hay fire, hay fire, get the hogs out first." As the team of horses and wagon stopped at a safe distance from the fire, my eyes filled with smoke but also with the excitement and wonder of this long-awaited dream. Grandpa was there along with other fathers and their sons. The long line of hand-over-hand bucket brigade began. I sat on the wagon and watched with excitement but also sadness. The hogs were saved, but there was no saving the barn. Several farmers were brave risking possible injury and burns. They had used all the water. The barn burned to the ground that night. I rode home with Grandpa in the Model T, the odor of my clothes telling where I had been. The long-awaited experience with Grandpa was over. I needed only once to feel the excitement, sadness and the love of neighbors for each other.

My grandmother was also hard working. Yet she always had time to teach me how to sew and cook. I learned how to cook on a wood-burning stove, making everything from bread to country-fried chicken in an iron skillet. I never knew my grandmother to have recipes. She just cooked, and it was always delicious. The most special food I learned to prepare was the fried chicken. It is still a favorite in my family. The secret to cooking on the wood stove was acquiring and maintaining the right temperature, allowing the wood to burn down, having hot embers and the iron skillet piping hot with shortening. On the farm, we used fresh rendered lard. Of course, the other secret was fresh chicken. Often Grandma would choose a young one from the chicken house and dress it the day before. They were referred to as "spring fryers." Nothing could compare with using the iron skillet with fresh lard on a wood stove. It made the chicken evenly browned, crispy and tender.

My delight was to get in the old Model T Ford and go to the mill to buy chicken feed. The back seat was removed to make room for the various things we took to sell at the market. It was a funny, bumpy old car. Grandpa kept it polished for the Saturday trip to town. The chicken feed was bagged in multicolored floral cotton sacks. Grandma would let me pick three or four prints of my choice. We emptied the feed into large buckets when we got home. After washing the sacks, ripping the seams, pressing and folding very neatly, I packed them carefully in my suitcase to take home. They would be ready for my mother to make my dresses for school. I often sketched designs for my dresses, my mother would cut a pattern and then sew them. Sometimes she would add a bit of lace that Grandma sent home with me.

I always took two dresses to my grandparents for the summer. They were for Sunday! Every Sunday, while Grandma was in church service, I was in Sunday school. She gave me ten pennies for my offering. I carried them in a special black velvet purse. There was a large white wooden replica church with a majestic steeple that stood in the middle of the Sunday school classroom. When it was time for the offering, we all made a circle around the church with our offerings in hand. As we sang "Jesus Loves Me" and walked around the church, we dropped our coins in the slot in the steeple. You could only put one coin in at a time. I was so thrilled I had ten because I could keep walking so many times around and keep singing. I loved to sing, and it seemed the sun always shined when we were in that room. I was happy there.

My brother spent most of the summer helping at my uncle's farm nearby. He worked hard helping the threshing crew and chores. We were six and eight years of age when we started our trips for the summer. It continued on for four years. Our work ethic was acquired at a young age, and we never regretted it. For my daily work on the farm, I gathered eggs, milked cows, fed chickens, picked berries, weeded the garden, and much more. Work was a part of my life, and it always was intertwined with overwhelming love. As the hay was mowed, berries dried up, squash was ready to gather from the vines, and the garden was dying off, I knew summer's end was near. A sadness always came over me. The vision of the brown suitcase in my father's hand returned so vividly. Often, I cried myself to sleep at night as I counted the days I had left to stay with my grandparents.

Many daughters grow up wanting to marry a husband with qualities like their father. I wanted someone like my grandfather. He had patience, dependability, good humor, and he knew life was more valuable than the dollar. I would dream of finding someone who recognized my worthiness, my kindness, and my fun-loving personality. I loved to laugh, and Grandpa would laugh with me. We could make a joke out of anything when we were together.

He had made stilts for me to walk out in the chicken yard and chicken house to gather eggs. I didn't like walking in chicken manure, so I put a basket on my arm, walked on stilts, and gathered eggs. I got pretty good at it. One day he said, "Hey, Topsy, if you get good enough on those stilts, we could get you in the circus." It was a silly thought, but we laughed, and I often dreamed of what it would be like in a circus as I gathered eggs. Life was positive when I was in their home.

When I was ten years old and my brother was twelve, we stayed without a sitter on the family acreage while both our parents worked in town. Summers spent with our grandparents were over. We walked along the highway and then a country road to our one-room country schoolhouse. We had a few chickens and pigs to care for after school, and I prepared most of the evening meals. I loved music and somehow "fate" came knocking when a music studio owner knocked on our door one Saturday morning. She was selling accordion lessons.

She looked so happy and with a big smile she said, "I'm looking for children or adults who would like to do something fun. Do you have children?" Luckily my mother was home from work that day, and I begged her to sign me up. She agreed it would be wonderful if I could have this opportunity. But when my father heard about it, he said, "No, you must go earn your own money for that." So, I got a job housecleaning and babysitting with a nearby farm family to pay for lessons and rented accordion. My mother secretly handed me coins to supplement what I didn't have before each lesson.

Saturday was my music lesson day. I carried my small twelve-base accordion in what seemed like an oversize case. It was heavy, but I was proud and determined to carry it into the studio. My lessons were always prepared well for I loved to practice. This music was now a part of my life, a positive portion in days of turmoil.

Money was always an issue at our house. But my mother's soothing words were, "As long as we have two nickels to rub together, we will be fine, Carole." There was always a shortage in the budget because too much went for my father's liquor. It's one thing to be poor and happy. It's another to be poor and unhappy. Music became my passion as an escape to happiness. Often, I prayed I could just get lost in music. I wanted to wander into a deep forest and just sing and dance. I envisioned playing, dancing, singing and being among flowers in a grassy meadow.

What would satisfy my soul? I was searching. Isn't there more to look forward to than making meals for the family at ten years old and struggling to escape the physical blows from my father? What do I want to be when I grow up? Will I find someone like my grandfather to marry?

We moved a short distance away to a small town with a population of 300 to 500. My parents bought the general store. There was not enough money to buy both the business and a house. So, they purchased a small used travel trailer and parked it on the lot beside the general store. My parents and I slept in the trailer. My brother slept alone in a small back room of the store. My father continued working in town while my mother, brother, and I managed the store. Besides the groceries, we had a single gas pump and post office. My mother was the postmistress.

The two-room schoolhouse, for kindergarten through eighth grade, was only a block away from the store. I was now in fifth grade, my brother in seventh. After eighth grade, we would attend high school in a larger town. But it was at this small elementary school where I met a very dear friend who has made an impact on my entire life.

She preferred to be addressed as "Mrs. Pauline," and she taught many years at this school. She was married to a carpenter, and they lived a short distance from the school. She was a tall lady, well-rounded, and ever so neatly dressed in simple designs, flattering and pleasing. At school, she wore a fragrance that gave the classroom a fresh, clean aroma, overcoming the odor of the wood-burning stove. Her smile, beneath her wire-rimmed glasses, was framed by her short, curly, graying hair. When she hugged us at the end of the day, her body radiated love. From the first day in school, I knew I could confide in her.

Mrs. Pauline had an outstanding intuition. She was astutely aware of any conflict in the homes of her students. She always had a listening ear and words of wisdom. She had comforted me and dried my tears many times. One autumn day, after she gave me her end-of-the day hug, she whispered, "Carole, come and visit me Saturday morning at 10:00 AM. I have a surprise for you."

"What could the surprise be?" I wondered. "It's not my birthday or a holiday." On Saturday morning, Blondie, her cocker spaniel, met me at the door. Across the room, beautiful pieces of crystal and a chest of silverware sat on the dining room table. It looked like she was in the midst of serious housecleaning.

"OK, Carole," Mrs. Pauline said, "This is what would really help me out in keeping up with teaching and the housework. I trust you because I know you've worked a lot and understand the importance of doing a good job." She continued by saying, "Every Saturday, I would like for you to come and wash my china and polish my silver. Then I would like you to place it neatly back in the china cupboard. You can do this while I am in the kitchen cooking. I will pay you $2.00 every Saturday. Would you like to do this for me?"

I was in shock and dismay. "Why would she trust me with her very best crystal and silver? What if I broke one of the treasures?" With a deep breath and feigned confidence, I said, "Yes, Mrs. Pauline. I would be so very proud to help you." We hugged. I knew I had a friend for life.

Spending Saturday mornings with Mrs. Pauline was special. As I polished and washed these treasures, I shared my home life of turmoil with her. As a child, my self-esteem was extremely challenged, for I was surrounded with alcohol and abuse. Mrs. Pauline constantly praised me and taught me values that would last me a lifetime. As I look back on this now, I know this job was a pretext for the real reasons for me to be there. Mrs. Pauline brought guidance and purpose into my life. Every Saturday, as I finished lunch and felt her loving hug, she said, "Remember, Carole, "You can do anything you want. Just go forward. It will be there and remember, you must always forgive."

Why should I forgive my father? I thought he was the one who should ask for forgiveness. My journey to adulthood had just begun. Learning how to forgive, let go of anger, and feel the grace of God were giant steps in my recovery.

Once I started music lessons, I no longer went to visit Mrs. Pauline on Saturdays. Adel, my music instructor, hired me to babysit and do house cleaning for her in exchange for music lessons. Going to her home on Saturday was special. I loved caring for their little girl and cleaning the house. Saturday was dance night so at the end of the day, Adel and her husband went to a ballroom dance and took me with them. As a young girl, I learned to dance in this Czech community, and loved it.

Upon entering high school, I focused on studies and had entertainment gigs with my accordion, sometimes getting as much as $10.00 an event. I worked part time at a bakery, and several times a week at a soda fountain. During the summers I was a carhop for the A&W Root Beer. I told my classmates I was really too busy to socialize. Basically, I was too embarrassed to take friends home to see my father's actions. Singing in the school choral was my only activity with classmates. Church was a huge support, giving me confidence that I was a good person. I also sang in the church choir. But at sixteen, I struggled to understand this thing about forgiveness. Why did I have to forgive my dad for abusing me?

My high school years overflowed with turmoil. My older brother served in the Army after high school. I missed him. We were a support for one another. During this time, we also moved from place to place. Several times we were evicted because of delinquent rent. When I saw the police car pull up in front of the house, I knew once again we would have to move. It was always the same routine. Once I saw the car, I would have time to hide behind the sofa. The police officer would gather his papers in the car and then slowly approach our door. Since my parents worked, I was most often alone when he arrived. I would stay hidden until he left. I always told my mother, not my father, about it because I knew he would be angry. After some attempts at delivering the notice, they always managed to evict us. We would move again.

Eventually my parents divorced. My passion for music provided an escape that was sadly pushed down inside me when my father told me I couldn't make money teaching music. I had no funds for college. In those days a woman either got married or became a schoolteacher, a secretary or a nurse. I got married.

# Marriage

My brother had several friends from high school. John stood out as rather special to me in the group. He and my brother had both served in the Army after high school. I knew him as one of my brother's friends, but when he returned from the service, our relationship soon became romantic.

He grew up in a well-established farming family. Since I had spent so much time on my grandparent's farm, I was happy and comfortable spending time with his family. I liked his mother, and she always had some snack to send home with me. I quickly fell in love with him and his family. We had many conversations about our future. His father didn't believe in college, and I wouldn't be going either, since I didn't have the money to attend.

In October, after graduating from high school in the spring, he said, "Honey, I have an idea. I will work for a while on the farm until I get a job in town. Then, when I save up enough money, we will get married. Will you marry me?" I was in love. This life looked much better than the one I had been living. I said, "Yes. And I can get a job, too. I know how to work."

When we got married, we didn't have much money, a common occurrence with newlyweds starting out. But, despite our lack of money, I had a much more comfortable life than the one I had experienced growing up. I felt grateful and always went the extra mile to please my in-laws. At their large family gatherings, I always brought a basket of homemade food. As the years went by, it seemed more and more was expected of me. Often, I helped my mother-in-law can and freeze foods from the garden. After all, I was "the girl from the other side of the tracks," as they said in those days. I felt I had to prove myself, even though they loved and accepted me. They didn't have a daughter, so I felt special and protected from gossip regarding my dysfunctional family. I focused on being successful with my office job and with being a good wife. My husband worked on the farm with his parents and eventually left to work in town. He completed business college and became very successful in the corporate world. His goals were never about farming, but rather to climb the corporate ladder.

For me, each of these transitions—graduating from high school, getting married, having in-laws, working in an office, dealing with my parents' separation, and becoming a mother—all felt like giant steps. But I did it. I was happy and in love with my husband and with a new life as a mother to our son. In the next six years, we were blessed with two daughters. I left the office job and taught accordion lessons while raising our children.

# Career

After ten years of marriage, my husband and I often discussed my early desires for a nursing degree. We had built a new home; I was very happy teaching accordion lessons as I raised our family. We were a team. When we got married, I thought I wanted a nursing profession. But now I was so in love with being a mom and having a beautiful family. I was proud and determined to have a stable family full of love.

One day my husband said, "You need to go to college and make some real money. You always wanted to be a nurse." Again, it felt like it was something someone else wanted me to do. "Make some real money?" I asked, "Where will the money come from to go to college? I don't want you to make that decision for me."

Now, after three children, I wondered if nursing was still my passion. I was dedicated to our family and wanted to be there for them. I was determined to give my children much more than what I had known. I said, "But now we have a family. I want to be with our family. I can wait and go to college later." At this point, my children were preteens and teenagers. I wanted to be with them during this time. I had several discussions with my husband about it, and each time he strongly emphasized how much more I could make as a nurse.

I asked myself, "Perhaps being a nurse is my journey in life. But is it too soon?" I had many doubts if I could balance responsibility of wife, mother, and student of a demanding education. Remembering those words, "You Can Do Anything You Want to Do." I decided to go for it. I registered in nursing school. Studies began. For several months, I continued to teach music lessons to help fund my college tuition. I could not have accomplished it without the support of the whole family. With books piled high on the dining room table, my kids and I did homework together. The demands were often overwhelming. I had to convince myself I was doing it for myself, not for my husband's desire for financial gain. I have never regretted the decision, but I have always told myself it was MY journey.

As the years progressed, I found myself drawn to oncology nursing. Chemotherapy was new in our community at that time. I studied all the treatments and types of cancer, finding a real passion in caring for the patients enduring this disease. My work involved caring for cancer patients in the hospital, administering chemotherapy in clinics and teaching nursing students. It was not uncommon to sit at the bedside of a terminal patient and assist through the dying process, supporting the patient and families. There were jubilant times as well, when news of a patient's recovery spread among our staff. The cancer unit was dear to my heart.

I was a member of the planning committee to open this section of the hospital. The American Cancer Society honored me with the "Nurse of Hope" award. This platform provided me the opportunity to deliver messages through workshops around the country, sharing an optimistic perspective on cancer and prevention.

I created and presented an educational program for preschool and elementary children, "Kathy Healthy Chew," that focused on eating healthy at a young age and avoiding tobacco in all forms. Dressed in an apple costume, I visited elementary school classrooms, delivering this message of health for the children as well as reaching out to their parents. Caring and teaching was a major part of my life. These twenty-five years teaching and assisting oncology specialists, helped prepare me for future challenges in life.

# Working the Marriage

Marriage requires many compromises. Financial management is vital to be successful. My husband sought financial fortune, while I tried my best to be an exemplary caregiver, mother, wife, wage earner, and home-maker. It left me little room to find out who I really was. I was told, "Your paycheck, Honey, goes in the bank. I will tell you what you can spend." My husband made comments like, "Be glad you are a nurse. It is financially so much better than teaching accordion in our home." I began questioning whether or not our goals were mutual in the marriage. My husband was determined that I could provide a second income for our family as well as be a wife and a mother. I liked my nursing career, but I was exhausted and torn apart playing too many roles. Besides that, he didn't see any problem with him controlling all the money I made as a nurse!

One day I said, "I am wearing too many hats. I'm the wife of a corporate manager, expected to entertain with banquets; a mother of three children, tasked with caring for a home including cleaning, laundry, grocery shop-ping, baking, and cooking all meals; and finally, have a career as a full-time nurse! Not only that, I have to strictly follow the budget you make." I felt like I was going to run out of breath detailing all of these assigned duties. Then I said, "I do not know who I am anymore or who I was meant to be or who I want to be. I have no time to enjoy what we have. We have become a machine, accumulating money without any meaning." He said, "We are doing what all families do when they are working and raising a family. We are making money to be able to do things." "Money!" I screamed, "Either there is not enough or there is savings for something extraordinary. Where is the joy in the simple things of everyday life? I don't have to travel the world." I needed space. My soul was searching for a peaceful green meadow. I felt like I was being trampled by demands.

The role of being a good mother and companion was far more important to me than making a huge salary and building our bank account. My husband was determined to be financially successful. For him, success was annual extravagant vacations. Each one was bigger and better and designed to show off his success to his fellow workers and friends. Certainly, I learned wonderful things traveling to worldwide places, but I often said, "Let's just do something simple and go to a theatre performance." But when he decided to travel far and wide, I dutifully gave in. I only enjoyed the simple things when I was alone.

I was on a spiritual journey of growth and finding my authentic self. As a mother, a wife, and a registered oncology nurse, I found myself stretched in various directions. When I traveled presenting seminars as Nurse of Hope for the American Cancer Society, I gained a great deal of insight into people and their families. I earned the respect from the professional world as well as the families. It was heartwarming to see the joy these people found in each day. I could relate to them the pleasures they saw in sunrises and smiles on children's faces. It is something that cannot be taught. I hoped my husband would discover the joy of simple things but the blinders he wore wouldn't allow it.

I felt in control when I was working, but a loss of control at home. My paycheck was deposited into investments and I was told exactly what I was allowed to spend beyond that. My husband said, "I will take care of the financial planning. You were not in charge of the money in your family. How would you know how to manage it now?" I followed his orders, but I felt things were out of balance and not in my favor!

Having grown up with very few material things and very little happiness, all I wanted was a hug and be told, "I love you." I felt like I was still treated like the little girl who hid in the corner for fear of punishment. When I asked my husband to be a partner in making decisions for our family, I was always totally ignored. I was intelligent. Why didn't I have a voice that mattered? Why couldn't we be a team?

No matter what we were doing, celebrating holidays and birthdays, traveling, camping, hunting, or fishing, we looked like the happiest of families. My children always showed me unconditional love. The view from outside was "the perfect marriage." Our friends saw our lovely home. Our kids often invited friends over to share meals, play games, and just hang out. We had neighborhood parties on our deck. What could be wrong in this family?

But inside I was empty. I had no self-worth, and I was unhappy. I had been a people pleaser since a child. If I didn't go along with what they wanted, the outcome was never pleasant. I was still a people pleaser. When would I please myself?

Often, I wanted to visit my mother who had remarried and moved to another state. My husband always found a reason why a trip south to visit my mother wasn't convenient or in the budget. He said, "She moved there. Let her come visit you." I always gave in because it was easier than trying to deal with his temper. It hurt to hear him speak unkindly about my parents. He had not walked in my lonely shoes. At these moments, I felt I was revisiting the painful moments of my childhood.

Years passed. My mother's husband died with cancer. Just a few years later she died alone in the emergency room with pneumonia. My mother always appeared young and vibrant. She was still working full time at age sixty-eight. It was hard to believe she would no longer be there for our Saturday morning phone calls. I missed those adult mother-daughter conversations.

# Without a Voice

Happiness is recognizing your soul and loving yourself. How did I lose my voice? When did I learn I was supposed to be quiet and follow a man's directions no matter what I thought? Looking back, it probably started when I was a child and my mother would buy the weekly issue of *Hit Parade* magazine for me. I loved memorizing and singing all the songs. Coming into the house, my father would yell, "You are singing and memorizing those stupid songs again. Throw that magazine away. I don't know why your mother buys one every week. It's a waste of money. We don't have money to spend on foolish things. There are more important things to do here." I hid my magazine behind the sofa, so it wouldn't be destroyed. Then I whispered and sang softly to myself, "I'm Going to Buy a Paper Doll to Call My Own." It was one of my favorites.

Years later when I was a mother myself working alone in my kitchen, the music from the radio soothed my overworked body. Our children were grown and gone now to create their own families. But music still took me to far-off places of stillness where I could discover and create. I danced around the room; sometimes I envisioned it a ballroom, other times a meadow with many flowers. I knew I would have that solitude a few more hours before my husband came home from his many fishing trips. Sometimes I sang, but most often, I just felt the freedom of dancing and imagining myself as a graceful angel. I was never with anyone. I just experienced the freedom of dancing and moving with the air and sunshine.

Often, he would come in from the garage, walk to the radio and turn it off. "Why do you always have the radio blaring in the house? It's distracting to have music on all the time. You could be thinking about more constructive things," he said. "What have you been doing all day?"

"Oh," I said, "You would be proud of me. I worked on our grocery budget and household needs."

"You will never get that figured out," he said. What do you know about finances? Your family knew nothing about finances. They lost everything. That will not happen with my management."

My husband's impatience and lack of appreciation for my interests and my talents sent me emotionally right back to those times when I was listening to my father say similar things and crouching in fear behind my parents' couch. At times I felt that leaving my life behind sounded better than living it. I realized I had dropped to the very bottom of muddy waters. I felt it was time for me, actually both of us, to seek counseling.

How do you explain that the marriage isn't working after forty-plus years, and you no longer can carry on? Disagreements became more and more prevalent. I was becoming more conscious of my own needs, wishes, talents, and opinions and started speaking up for myself. Pleasing myself became more important but clashed with the people pleaser I had been. It became obvious to me I needed to communicate my feelings to my husband, but it felt increasingly difficult to keep harmony between us.

To the outsider, our marriage appeared as icing on a cake—always smooth and unblemished. I need not elaborate regarding the causes of my failed marriage. In a partnership, neither wife nor husband are without shortcomings. For me, I needed space to live the life my soul had been sent on earth to do. Did I know at the time what it was? Perhaps not, but for years, I was living and following the journey of the life someone wanted me to follow. I knew I had to find my authentic self. One day it became clear to me that I must leave.

# Forgive

I've always had a vivid memory of my father's death on Christmas Eve. It turned out that one of my former students was his nurse that night. My father's health had declined, and in spite of all the anger through the years, I was now at his bedside watching him suffer over the past few days. My brother sat beside me. I wondered if his memories raced through his mind as they were in mine. Was it time to forgive? I remembered the words my fifth-grade teacher always said: "You must forgive."

Through the years, after he quit drinking and smoking, my father and I had talked about things. He never apologized for all the early years of abuse. I always wondered, did he not know the impact it had on my brother and me, or was it too difficult to say, "I'm sorry"?

Our family had a German tradition of oyster stew on Christmas Eve. My father wanted us to be together for the evening. As a nurse, I knew the signs nearing death. It would be soon. If I was to ever forgive him, it must be verbalized now. In a weak voice, he said, "Run along now." This was a phrase he used since I was a child. The family left the room. I lingered and gave the nod to my former nursing student to keep him comfortable with the morphine. I took his hand, gave him a kiss, and said, "I forgive you, Dad, for all the things that hurt us so much, and you didn't know how to handle." He whispered, "I'm sorry. I love you."

We made our way home for the oyster stew that he wanted us to enjoy that Christmas Eve. The phone call came from the hospital as we sat down to eat. He had taken his last breath. Both of us took charge of our feelings.

I was able to forgive him, and he apologized and expressed his love for me. My relationship with him was complete.

# Take Charge

Several years later on Christmas Eve I knew I had to take charge once again. Where would I go? What would I do? I had not prepared myself for this moment, but it came over me like a flash of light, opening a new world. "You Can Do Anything You Want to Do."

After a painful childhood and forty-seven years in a controlling marriage, my soul was crying to be recognized. My talents had been locked inside me, undiscovered and crying to reveal themselves. I had been living someone else's life. Certainly, I had loved my husband, the father of our children. But we had different ideas about success. He measured it in financial gains, while my soul longed for the little things in life. His big picture was too powerful and large to recognize the small portions on the canvas that pleased me. Just as the lotus flower rises and blooms above the murky waters to achieve its serenity and beauty, I needed to rise above troubled waters and align with the Universe. Like the forgiveness I gave my father, I needed to forgive my husband and move forward to answer my soul's calling.

# Feeling a Loss

Eckhart Tolle describes essence as the "vital formless dimension of who you are." He prefers to call it, "Being, which is prior to existence." He goes on to describe how people are so engrossed in the content of their lives, on what is happening and what may happen, that they have forgotten eternity, which is their origin. They have become hypnotized by all the world's changing and challenging events that they have forgotten who they are and what their purpose is. He further states, "Eternity is the living reality of who you are." At one point, I started golfing several days a week. It gave me joy and kept my mind focused. I met a new golfing partner, Zee. She was recently widowed and finding her space in the single world. We shared our personal lives and became very good friends.

One day, I said, "Zee, I've been in marriage counseling for some time now. It's not working. It was difficult to get him involved in counseling in the first place. He doesn't want to continue anymore. I think I need to move out and then see if we can work things out."

"That might be a good idea," she said. "Get a fresh look at things."

We sat in the clubhouse having a cold drink after our round of golf. Without hesitation, Zee at once said, "You don't have to worry about where to go. When you're ready to leave, you can stay with me. I have lots of room. You can think over your final decision once you separate." Her comforting words offered me a great peace of mind. I wanted to continue counseling. But just that very day, my husband had said, "This counseling is of no value. I'm done with it." Zee's offer was exactly what I needed at that moment.

I made the temporary move to her home, giving me space to work through my decision. I continued to work with my counselor to make the final decision to end my marriage. The counselor advised me the chances of reconciling were slim.

Zee was very accommodating. "Sleep in, Carole," she'd say. "The house is yours. Enjoy the solitude and relax." Living in Zee's home provided me time to sort out my feelings and make a decision that would have profound implications for me and my family. Eventually, I worked through the agonizing decision to leave my husband and seek the life that was calling my soul.

O   O   O

Leaving a marriage that many friends and relatives saw as solid and happy, felt like I was removing a huge chapter of my life—the good memories as well as the not-so-good memories and sadness about losing family get-togethers and that bond.

Our adult, married children felt the loss and had a hard time understanding the reasons behind this huge change. "What is happening?" they all asked. "We didn't know you were unhappy." During the course of our marriage counseling, I tried to help my grown children understand that through the years, people sometimes grow apart. I had done a good job of protecting my children, my grandchildren, and myself. There had been so many wonderful family times together. They often asked, "After over forty years together, why can't it work out?" In numerous conversations with them, I tried to describe my struggle against being controlled. Years passed with healing and understanding, but of course not without challenges. The rock-solid home foundation crumbled. As parents, we walk different paths and contribute from our individual souls. Over time, my children slowly became aware of my need to be "me." I had to exit the marriage to find my true essence.

# Search for
# Happiness

I moved to Park City, Utah to be near one of my daughters and start a new life. I had my own condo in the Wasatch Mountains, a refreshing environment full of sunshine. My daughter had sidelined her nursing career to become an entrepreneur. She and her family happened upon a European deli for sale, bought it, and started a new venture in Salt Lake City.

This delightful gem, with limited seating, was located along other retail establishments in this upscale strip mall. If you walked down the sidewalk, you would see similar storefronts. However, when you approached this business, the sign, JUHL HAUS, would grab your attention. There you would find a colorful display window with German mugs, jars of jams, and candy. Mouthwatering smells of food floated out from cracks around the door. It would draw you in to take a look.

When you stepped through the door, you felt as if you had trekked through Germany, Switzerland, Italy, or any number of places in Europe, and happened upon a special inn. It was just the place for a bowl of soup and to rest your weary feet. The pungent fragrances of salami, cheese, garlic, herbs, fresh baked goods, and chocolate filled the air.

Once inside, on the crude stone walls, you would see authentic European photos, luxuriously framed, of Neuschwanstein Castle, Danube River, and the scenic Alps towering above lazy cows grazing the meadows. Shelves from floor to ceiling were filled with packaged European special import foods. Cookware, linens, cookbooks and much more crowd the narrow aisles, encouraging you to keep winding through the shop. The intriguing displays with European packaging are so interesting, you will want to touch everything and read the labels of the not-so- everyday goods. Treasured vanilla beans hung inside their safely locked glass cases.

Chocolate candy wrapped in foils of bold colors would speak to you from several countries.

You would immediately want to sample them all and compare. Can you imagine this wondrous world seen through the eyes of children shopping with their parents?

Then your eye would be caught by the cheese and meat case. No less than fourteen feet in length or perhaps more, this refrigerated case held cheese from all around the world. Blues, Gorgonzola, Classico, Le Moulis, Cheddars, wheels of Parmigiano-Reggiano, Triple Crème Appenzeller, and many, many more stand in their respected place, waiting to be chosen. My daughter and granddaughters hand cut each cheese order. They also briefly shared the origin and story about the cheese being chosen. Special cheese knives lined the wall behind the cutting table. Each cheese selection was wrapped carefully in a specific manner to retain flavor and freshness. All around you, you would hear stories, laughter, and chatter from customers discussing what to get next time they embarked on this unique adventure. The storytelling became longer and longer and more interesting with each cheese purchased. The cheese counter was the focus of the shop with customers crowding around to hear the stories. Often the customer went home with an entirely different purchase because of the interesting history about the making of a specific cheese in a little-known village with goats or cows. It was a true European experience to visit the Juhl Haus.

But, wait, I have left out something very important; Flowers. Nothing was complete in this setting without flowers. With my German ancestry and creativity, our home had always been adorned with flowerboxes overflowing with huge geraniums, vines, and a colorful mixture of blooms. Creativity with planting and helping others with their arrangements was my passion.

With my daughter's ability and experience with floral arrangement, a

Munich, Germany atmosphere was created at the door of Juhl Haus. The entrance was framed with huge planters of bold red geraniums, white and purple petunias, and various vines with bits of yellow peeking from inside. The tiered planters with all of these colors welcomed you to a land beyond. Inside, small pots of forget-me-nots peeked out from behind dinnerware, a bouquet of daisies spoke from atop the cheese counter, and vines meandered through the most surprising places to intrigue the visitor.

In October, we celebrated Oktoberfest. In front of the shop, you would see the beer tent with a St. Pauli Girl greeting everyone and helping to pour beers. My son-in-law, wearing his Lederhosen and a German hat, would grill the brats. In my traditional dirndl German dress, I would play my accordion, and people on the streets would join in to joyously polka.

In the winter, the Juhl Haus came alive with a new look. Holly, evergreen, pine cones and a shimmer of tinsel adorned the window boxes, waiting for a dusting of snow. Often the pansies liked to peek out from beneath the bed of evergreen to say, "I don't always go away in the summer. Look at my sunshine now." Walking through the door, you would see pink, white, and purple cyclamen peeking from behind pickle jars and jams and even cookbooks. The traditional poinsettia was placed on the cheese counter. The word was out. Juhl Haus had a great food establishment and a floral shop!!

Orders for flower arrangements started flooding the Juhl Haus. A new business was born. My daughter and I worked together building the floral business. Eventually it became my project. It flourished quite rapidly and aided in my healing process of new beginnings.

The Wasatch Mountain homes with their Swiss elements of beauty was a welcoming haven for floral design of window boxes. I was in my element. The home owner's major interest was to have instant beauty in the mountains for the very short growing season. It became a challenge to create outstanding beauty to endure summer and continue into early season of frost.

Often, I extended sales by doing floral arranged containers for indoor decor. I lived in the beauty of the flowers, Wasatch Mountains, and Lambs Canyon.

In addition to helping at the Juhl Haus and attending to the floral business, I was able to spend time with my family. I golfed in the Park City area, hiked, experienced the snow shoe adventure over the trails and traveled in the nearby scenic areas. Traveling through the Lambs Canyon between Park City and Salt Lake City gave me a peace and healing. Life was good.

# Jake

Jake was over six foot, with posture straight as an arrow. In his early seventies, he was strong, trim, and walked with a proud character. His thinning salt-and-pepper head of hair was becoming with his well-groomed matching mustache. His hands were always warm. They had a healing touch. His kind soul was hidden behind his ever so slight smile and quiet demeanor. Over the years, people may have thought he was unfriendly because he smiled so little. In our years together, Jake shared with me his theory of why this was so. He said, "My father told me when I was very young that my smile was not very becoming and that I should not put on big smiles." I thought Jake's smile was infectious in drawing others to him, and in later years being together, it became more a part of him. When we danced, he truly smiled.

We met as coworkers in a resort complex in Texas. He was an outside restaurant consultant from Canada, currently there for the winter. As this was a Canadian-owned resort, he was able to be employed as a fellow Canadian.

My husband and I were there for our usual "Snow Bird" stay. We were also in the middle of marriage counseling. I had always worked at the same job during our winter vacations. I was a resort dining hostess and managed the servers.

It was a busy winter. I worked four days a week in the restaurant as well at teaching aqua aerobics at the resort. Being with our longtime friends and trying to rebuild my marriage was also my focus. In my heart, I knew the marriage was over, even though my mind tried to work it out.

Jake and I worked as a team in the dining room, bringing new ideas, a change of menu, and lots of laughter and joy. We had a connection and a respect for one another that bonded the entire establishment. He shared his stories of years in the restaurant business with all of the staff. His many years before retirement included owning a small coffee shop, a drive-in sandwich-and-fries shop (the first in Canada), and a fine dining evening establishment. He brought fresh ideas to this restaurant and implemented many improvements. The end of the season came and we each went our separate ways.

Located in Park City, divorced, working the floral business and enjoying my family, I still recalled the warm sincerity and respect I had felt from Jake. Was it serendipity that I had met him years before? I made a phone call letting him know my sequence of events. With his RV, some weeks later he traveled from Canada to visit and stayed at an RV park nearby. Our friendship grew deeper. Ontario and Utah are many miles apart resulting in long treks and limited time together. I wanted to take time to readjust after long years of marriage, but I also was very fond of him and wanted to be with him. At last, I felt some happiness and love.

Many years of marriage, good or bad, results in adjustments for the entire family. The acceptance of someone new coming into the mix does not always take place easily, sometimes not at all. It was a challenge for my family to see someone else with me other than their father. But I felt relief from the secret bondage I had been in for many years, which had been a well-kept secret from outsiders.

My flower business flourished. Jake came to stay for a summer to help. Having built a small portable greenhouse on my daughter's patio, we developed a real system. Our new cocoa-and-cream colored Chevrolet Avalanche traveled every week down the mountain to Salt Lake City. After carefully making our selections, we completely loaded up our Avalanche with flats of wholesale flowers, soil, fertilizer, window planters and pots. We designed, planted, delivered and attached our designs to homes and businesses. Our worktable was on the patio, in the valley of the Wasatch mountains. We were often presented with the challenge of saving our flowers from the nibbling moose. If we weren't careful, our worktable was their dining table. Their munching could destroy profit very quickly.

As a team, we found great satisfaction in working with soil and creating beauty. Jake used his carpentry abilities to attach the window boxes to homes and businesses. At summer's end, he would return to Canada and visit his family while I remained in Utah. As spring would burst forth in the valley, once again my thoughts turned to purchasing flowers and products. The spring and summer season are very short, therefore plans for the planting season started well in advance. I was always eager to acquire new clients and create individual arrangements especially for their home or business. The ragged, majestic peaks of the Wasatch Mountains and the rolling hills of Lambs Canyon fueled my desire to create.

Jake had always wanted a Jeep. So, when he visited Ontario in the fall, he bought a new black-and-tan Jeep Renegade. I knew he would really be proud driving around in snow-covered Utah. Arriving in late winter, he still had time to play before spring plantings.

He was on his way back to Park City, driving the new Jeep, when I received his phone call. "Carole," he said, "I am still going to visit my brother before I return, but I am not feeling just right. I think I should see a doctor when I get to Park City. Would you please make an appointment?" I was quite surprised and immediately alarmed, for he had never been ill. Now in his early seventies, he had never been hospitalized except in his early teens for gall bladder removal. He was a healthy man. I said, "What problems are you having? Tell me how you feel." He hesitated. After a few moments, he quickly responded with, "Oh, you know, maybe it's just the Jeep being a little rough riding. My kidney area feels tender. I think I will be ok." We talked a few minutes about the new Jeep, his trip, and when he would arrive. Nearing the end of the conversation, I said, "Just to be safe, I will make an appointment." "OK," he said, sounding relieved, "Maybe it would be best."

Upon having tests, waiting a couple days, and then consulting with the doctor, we learned that Jake had bladder cancer. We were barely six months into our new life together. It felt like a very harsh jolt. Since Jake was Canadian, he needed to make the trip back to Ontario. Evaluation and treatment were inevitable and should take place very soon.

Now all new challenges faced us—the Canadian winter, discouraging medical records, the selection of a Canadian oncology doctor, sharing the uncertainties of Jake's future with family, and realizing that we needed to implement a dramatic change in lifestyle. Remarkably, Jake took it in stride, and we persevered. We were determined to overcome the obstacles before us. With tests revealing a cancerous tumor within the bladder, small and hopefully slow growing, Jake chose to "wait and see." There were many agonizing decisions to be made. He would be financially compelled to have treatment in Canada unless he could afford care in the United States without insurance.

Another year in the floral business and several trips between Canada and the states convinced us a warmer climate would be a better choice than the brutal winters of Utah and Canada. The sunshine of Arizona laced with the return trips to his Ontario residence and medical evaluation would be an easier journey. We became a couple and acquired a second home in Arizona. Our love for each other grew stronger as we met obstacles head on and lived each day to the fullest.

Despite the many eventual cancer treatments in Canada, Arizona, and investigational treatment in California, we lived with a passion for life. In Jake's early years, he had taught dancing at Arthur Murray. Ballroom dancing was also my passion. We were together in our own world on the ballroom floor. Jake's tall, distinguished stature set him apart when we moved in and around other dancers. But it was our souls connecting that really distinguished us from everyone else. Often others would clear the floor to observe us dance. We weren't performing. It was our bond with one another! As we danced, we felt like we truly were two people appearing as one. Our souls seemed to speak to each other. I felt like an angel had been given a special blessing. I was always in the moment. The feeling remains with me always.

We took on the challenge of cooking a healthy diet and various other holistic approaches, trying desperately to beat the devastating disease. Jake would say, "Throw everything in that blender: fresh fruits, vegetables, proteins, and flax seed, we got this licked." We held respect and love for each other that kept us anchored in recognizing the beauty of each day.

Jake had great admiration for Clint Eastwood. He had seen every one of his movies and several more than once. Many of Clint's quotes were tucked in Jake's books just inside the cover. One of the quotes he definitely lived by and reminded me of often is: "The main thing is not how long you are on the planet, but the quality you have while you are here." Together with this philosophy and the outstanding patience Jake had, I lived a quality life at a slower pace. Another quote of Clint's that Jake lived by is: "The reason I don't retire is that I learn something new every day—it's about expanding, constantly pushing yourself." Reading was Jake's way of staying abreast of what was happening around him and learning. His faith was strong. He felt God was assisting him in carrying out his journey of life. He accepted what was before him.

Five years passed. His fatigue was more frequent. He was not driving. Trips back to Canada were more difficult. We still danced—slower, but together. Then it was more reading in his chair. Books he had collected for years took him to far off places in memory and fantasizing. The hospice doctor made frequent visits to our home to share Jake's latest reading. There were not a great deal of medical issues to attend to any longer, but the emotional support was invaluable. Upon the doctor's arrival, Jake would always greet him with, "Doc, come on in. We have lots to discuss. I have read three books since I last saw you. Where have you been?" The doctor would then rattle off a few reasons for being busy and finally say, "Just get with it. What have you read?" In chairs side by side in our library, they would converse about medical topics, distant lands, and life experiences. Jake had wanted to be a physician and read medical books much of his adult life. But what really captured the doctor's interest were the many humanistic stories of Jake's years as a restaurant entrepreneur. I believe it was therapy for them both.

Jake's family was in Canada, but he wanted to live his last days in our home in the sunshine state. Five years had passed. We could see those precious days were becoming fewer. Coming to the table for dinner had become extremely difficult.

After months of waiting, the dining room draperies I designed had finally just been hung. He said, "You know I will not be around much longer to enjoy them, but I will try to get to the dinner table tonight to see how beautiful they must be."

With his walker, which he totally disliked using, he made his way very slow and deliberately from the bedroom to the dining room table. So thin, he appeared even taller than his six foot plus. He ate very slowly and only a few bites. Pale in color and frail, he placed his hands on the arms of the chair and attempted to rise from the chair. He liked these chairs because they had large, easily moveable castors. However, this time, he lost his balance and tipped over onto the floor, where he lay in a curled-up position, I was horrified, scared, and at the same time also feeling guilty. He came to the table only to please me, to see the draperies. He said, "I'm ok. What the hell happened?" "Well, honey," I said," I think those castors you liked so well took you for a ride, and you couldn't hang on." I was concerned how I would get him up off the floor and back to bed. Yes, he had lost weight, but his six-foot frame would be a handful. Thinking I could get him into the wheelchair, which was lurking in the garage for just these emergencies, I headed to the garage and said, "Ok, Jake, I have an idea." All at once, he emphatically said, "Carole, NO WHEELCHAIR. I have not used one yet and don't want to now." Then quietly, as if thinking it through on how to get up, he said, "You know what my dad's advice was in emergencies like this?" Well, of course, my response was, "Having not known your father, I can't imagine. But I am really curious what can get us out of this predicament besides calling 911." With just a faint smile and a bit of enthusiasm still in his voice, he said, "Just get me a shot of scotch, let me sit here a minute, and then it will do wonders. Dad always said, 'Scotch never hurt anyone and can do a hell of a lot of good when you're in a jam.'" I took the best crystal glass from the cupboard, used only for scotch, and poured it with TLC. He sat on the floor and sipped. We laughed out loud at this whole scene. Looking around the room, slowly and with a slight smile, he said, "Honey, the draperies are beautiful. You will enjoy them long after I am gone." All because of these new draperies, he sat on the floor, sipping scotch, and wondering how to get back to bed. After a few minutes he said, "Alright, let's go for it." With a shot of scotch, willpower, and my helping hand, he made it into the chair with castors. I wheeled him back to bed. It was his last trip to the dining room. He never did get in that wheelchair.

Jake and I had been through five years of his cancer treatment. With thousands of miles traveling to and from Canada, Arizona, and weeks of treatment in California, he had made his decision where he wanted to spend his last days. He had discussed it with his children and was at peace. We were tightly bound together in love. He said, "I want to leave this life beside the best nurse in the world and dance out with the best dancer until I cross over." I was at his side to the last breath. I handed him to an angel who danced him over. No doubt he continues to dance with the angels on the other side. Occasionally I feel him tap me on the shoulder for a dance.

Little did I know the grieving and healing would be such a long process and lead to a devastating experience just three years later.

The five years with Jake were filled with joy as well as heartache. Jake's death from cancer was another adjustment on this journey. The grieving process was long and devastating. So many times, I tried to overcome the loss, but there was always something more I was reaching for. I had work, dance, design, travel, friends, financial stability, and health. What more did I need? I thought I wanted a companion like the one I lost. As I was to discover much later, what I needed the most was to love myself and elevate my self-esteem.

# Part 2

● ● ●

Online
Dating Scam

# Online Dating

Nearly two years had passed since Jake's death. I was not dating. Instead I golfed, participated in activities with women's groups, and took care of my home. I studied spiritual books, listened to webinars, and spent considerable time in spiritual growth studies.

I studied spirituality with various spiritual leaders: Mike Dooley, Jack Canfield, Eckhart Tolle, Gary Zukav, John Apollo, Tapping with Nick Ortner and others. Participating in spiritual growth webinars while attending classes gave me major strength for growth and balance. It helped me to become more grounded in spirituality and work through the grieving. However, joy was in and out of my life, never staying very long at a time. I knew grieving was still a part of my being, and it felt selfish. I know life ends at the right time for those leaving. But I certainly wasn't prepared for my companion to leave so soon.

I discovered hypnotism through the work of Lindsay A. Brady. His book, *As the Pendulum Swings,* helped me to eventually move forward with greater happiness. Lindsay described his book in the following way, "It is not just a book about hypnosis, but also a memoir about how my life has been transformed from one of fear, low self-esteem, guilt, and self-doubt into one of confidence, joy, and peace of mind by using the process called "hypnosis"—a process more accurately described by the word "perceptionism."[2] As I began to understand the mind/brain connection and how to remove the limitations we put on ourselves, I started to feel peace of mind and invite joy back into my life. Through this process, I moved towards a new beginning, participated in new activities, learned how to live in the NOW, and recognize the happiness in my life.

In doing so, I decided to study and become certified to teach the process of hypnotism. However, as I neared completion of the course and the exam, I felt uncertain about teaching others. I questioned if I wanted to again care and give to others with the amount of time that I had done in the past. It felt like this may lead me again to be a caregiver. I struggled with what I wanted to do and what I felt I should do. For some time, I did not realize that, my challenge was to love myself.

I also danced. Dancing had always been a part of my life. As a young girl, I went to the ballroom with my parents on Saturday night. My parents were active in social dancing and took me with them. As an adult, I attended ballroom classes for structured lessons. Learning advanced steps, how to waltz, foxtrot, swing, cha-cha-cha, rumba and other dances opened a new world. It was uplifting, excellent exercise, and it challenged my mind and body. Dancing had been such an important part of my relationship with Jake. Eventually, I started to compete in various ballroom competitions. I felt carried away in another world when I was on the dance floor. It led to new employment. I purchased a new gown for one of the competitions from Randall Designs, and they offered me a job. As sales manager, I traveled around the country to ballroom events, selling men and women's formal ballroom dance attire and assisting in the design of gowns. Competitive dancing and social dancing, traveling, and meeting people should have brought joy and happiness to my soul. However, life remained empty without companionship.

○   ○   ○

At one of the dance events, a long-time client, Nancy, asked, "Carole, do you have a gentleman friend?" I said, "No, I just haven't been out and around for dating. I'm just traveling for work and doing my dancing." I said, "It would be nice to meet someone, but there isn't much opportunity."

"Well," she said, "I think you should try online dating. I met my husband online, and we are very happy." I had met her husband, but I hadn't known how they had met. I told her, "Nancy, I will give it some thought. Is it easy to get started?" "Oh yes, Carole," she said, "Just pick an online service, you know there are many, enroll for a short time, and see what happens."

I started asking a few people at random what their opinion was about online dating. Everyone I asked either had not tried it or had met their spouse online. There was no negative feedback. I had spent little time on the computer other than for my job. Visiting online services or seeking information on dating had not been in my realm of interest. Three people had now shared with me that they had met their spouses online and were happily married. I was a bit uncomfortable about trying this, but I was hearing good things about it. So, after much thought, I said to myself, "Why not?"

I looked over a few online services and made my choice for eHarmony. I actually chose it because of the word "Harmony." It was rather stressful for me to enter the personal information, for I was hesitant to share. I entered very little detail about myself and enrolled for a minimal amount of time.

In a very short time, less than a week, I had many responses. I felt no interest in them and made no response. After about three weeks into enrollment, a gentleman showed interest in my profile, and he seemed of interest to me as well. As we corresponded through eHarmony, we decided to meet at a mutual place between our locations. We continued to date for dinners, outdoor activities, and some local travel. The more time we spent together, however, the less compatible we became. I felt restricted in sharing our interests, and common interests were few. We eventually went separate ways.

I returned to eHarmony. Again, there were many responses, but of little interest to me. Then a gentleman from out of state seemed like a good match. I was hesitant about meeting someone from out of state but decided to communicate. Eventually we met. We "cultivated" a friendship unique to us. He had many business responsibilities in his home state, and

I had a job. Neither of us was interested in relocating, but we developed a long-distance friendship. It was enjoyable to have phone conversations on many topics in our lives, and we gave each other support through various tragedies in our families. Life moved on. We both continued to look for the right companion while also keeping in touch as friends. My job kept me busy, but I had little social life. I was hoping for a dance partner, someone to share dinner and conversations. . . a companion. I really had all I needed but didn't realize it. I was slowly recognizing my own essence, but not totally—still searching for what I had with Jake.

I returned to eHarmony. My profile was still minimal, and I remained uncomfortable being online. Then an intriguing picture of a gentleman came up. It caught my eye. As I read his profile, it sparked my curiosity even more. He was born in Germany, liked to dance, widowed and without children, willing to relocate, liked to travel. It all seemed to fit my interests.

# Stolen Identity

I thought I prepared myself for a good experience meeting someone online. I performed an identity check on his online profile. He was from out of state, so I felt the need to investigate his profile before meeting him. He certainly had appeal, was the right age, had the same interests, and, most importantly, he interested me. So, I felt it could be worth the money for the search, and it gave me peace of mind. I told myself that I was doing everything necessary to continue communicating with him safely. He sent me his name, address, phone number, place of employment, wife's deceased name, German ancestry, and age. He also sent me online pictures, one a headshot close up, and another, a portrait in his home. He was a pleasant-looking gentleman, with that stout, strong European look I had seen so many times in Germany. I liked it.

Upon searching for his identity on Search Quarry, it became evident to me that he was in fact who he said he was. His German accent, along with being born and raised in Berlin, seemed legitimate. I traveled a great deal to Germany in the past and recognized the accent. There were times when I noticed the accent was not quite like I learned it, but different parts of the country have different dialects, so I brushed it off. Our mutual German ancestry was attractive to me. I felt we had something in common.

Several years ago, in a small town near Heidelberg, Germany called Mosbach, I located my ancestors' simple, two-story, wooden-framed home situated on a small lot. The yard was dotted with colorful floral plantings. A narrow stone walk, bordered with pink and white begonias, invited me to the front door.

Surprisingly, as I approached the house, I saw my family name painted on a shingle hanging near the door. It was a breathtaking moment to see the name on the house. The town crier had informed me all the family members were deceased. They were bakers for several generations. This tender moment has stayed with me and added to my attachment to Germany. I took several trips to various parts of Germany and feel a kinship to the country. This caused me to be particularly excited about meeting someone from Germany who could possibly be my new companion. The dating site seemed to be safe, and since Carl and I had several things in common, I felt quite comfortable continuing our communications online, but I also had some reservations. He was out of state and I really wanted to meet him. In spite of my nervousness, I moved forward. At the time, I was naive about the fact that information can be stolen online, and I had no idea our conversations could be a scam. I thought I had taken the necessary precautions to protect myself.

We continued talking online for about three weeks. Carl would often say, "Oh, I am so excited to meet you. I have been looking for just the right match. You have such a vibrant personality with so much energy. I really want to meet you." I asked about his work and what he liked to do when he wasn't working. I asked, "Do you go to movies, or dance?" He told me was a construction worker and his activities after work always matched my interests.

After three weeks, I received an email asking, "Hey, Carole, let's get out from under all the red tape with the online service. Let's go to our own emails. Wouldn't that be easier?" I was becoming quite interested in learning more about this gentleman. So, I said, "Sure, Carl, let's just use our own email addresses and drop the eHarmony for now."

I had not shared my adventure with any of my friends or family. By pursuing this adventure alone, I had no input or discussion from anyone. It was comfortable and I just wanted to enjoy the experience. I didn't feel like sharing it.

He had already discovered through our conversation many of my likes and little things about me. He would ask in his emails," What did you do today?" My response was always truthful, noting, "I had a client today in the shop who needed a new gown. It was fun to design and discover what she wanted. Tomorrow I will be packing for a business trip." Sometimes he would ask, "So, did you go out for lunch today?" What did you have?" Very quickly he knew much about my daily habits, routines, and the food I did or did not like. I told him my pleasures of life, without realizing how much I was sharing. He soon knew all about me, and he knew how to romance online. He began to address me with endearments, "Honey, Sweetie, My Love."

# Meeting

A month passed, and we still hadn't met. He wrote emails daily and phoned two to three times a week. His soft voice, with his German accent, was comforting and made me trust him. During one of his calls, I said, "Carl, when do you think we could arrange a meeting?" "Oh, Honey," he said, "It will be very soon, because I am really growing fond of you, and it seems we have so much in common. I really want to meet you in person. I thought about the travel that I needed to do for work. I asked him, "I am traveling to many places for my work. Could we meet for a day somewhere conveniently located?" Then his voice trailed off without interest in my question and said, "Let's just keep talking and sending emails for a while." His response bothered me, but I ignored it and continued to think of ways we could meet. We had many miles between us, but I had an idea.

I was traveling to visit my family for the Thanksgiving holiday through the Denver airport. There would be time between flights. I suggested we meet at the airport for lunch. With a considerable amount of time available, we could at least see each other and get a little better acquainted. We were both excited, and he was talking a great deal about our future together.

Carl told me many times that he wanted to retire from construction work. He said he needed one more contract to secure the finances for his retirement. His emails described the contract he was hoping to get, often stating how many long hours of negotiating he was doing, and what a large job it was. Carl became very emotional when he spoke of getting the contract and likened it to the future he had been planning with his wife before she died. The negotiations to secure the contract became a major discussion between us; however, I never learned any specifics about it only that it was in "construction."

Shortly before we planned to meet, he said, "This job is overseas and would put me in a position to leave all the hard labor behind and start us on the road to great fun together." I was taken by his interest in me, and completely unaware that overseas construction was the norm for online scamming. Initially he led me to believe it was a local contract. He didn't mention going overseas.

I believed the stage was being set for our future, but Carl was actually setting the stage for his scam. He told me he had lost his wife to cancer. They had no children. He was very excited hearing about my family, always wanting to know more and more about my children and grandchildren. Our conversations revolved around family. He was eagerly waiting to be a part of everything my family enjoyed. He knew how to romance me. He learned how important my family was to me. We shared our love of travel and where we would go. Both of us, of course, were interested in returning to Germany.

I daydreamed of our life together every time I received one of his emails. I could hear the bustle of people in Munich, my favorite city, and feel the vibration under my feet of the church bells ringing. Everything about Munich returned to my senses under its clear blue sky. The smell of the bratwurst sizzling at the street vendors' carts, tasting beer at the pubs, and dancing to the German music with brightly colored dresses everywhere. It was all so vivid. I imagined walking among the zillions of flowers blooming everywhere. It felt like a dream come true. I could taste the chocolate bars as we munched on them, walking hand in hand down the cobblestone streets. The mountains seemed to beckon me, "Come climb our peaks." I could feel the walk in the valley, hearing the cow bells clang, the copper bell tone sounding like no other. Oh, I was so thrilled at the thought of being in Germany with my new companion. I knew it would happen.

I shared my love for dancing and told him how pleased I was to have a partner again. What was there that would not be fun and special with this gentleman? He had already sent me flowers. Two romantic cards had arrived in the mail telling me how eager he was to meet me. Our meeting was to take place a few days after visiting my family for Thanksgiving. The date was set. We had the exact time and had chosen a lunch counter in the terminal. We each had a photo of each other. The time had finally arrived.

Black Friday, the day after Thanksgiving, I was on my way to our traditional Christmas shopping trip with my granddaughters. It was about a three-hour drive to the nearest large mall and, of course, a great adventure for all of us. A Girls Day!! I was not only excited about being with some of my family but also about meeting Carl the next day. It was a day filled with joy.

As we were driving, I received a phone call. It was Carl. His voice was soft and sweet as always, eager to know how I was. With apology and a tone of disappointment, he said, "I have been awarded the contract I have been waiting for. This will put us into a great retirement together. It will just be two-and-a-half months, no longer than three months that I will be out of the country. Then we will be set for a fabulous future together, Darling." He was going to Kuala Lumpur, Malaysia to work.

Having been to Kuala Lumpur in my travels, it all seemed very legitimate. I could feel, smell, and see the villages. The crowded narrow streets, winding around open-door shops, overflowed with small cars and food carts. Small neighborhoods of housing, seemingly patched together, bulged with two or three generations of families. I could imagine modern day construction necessary to improve businesses and homes.

The more Carl explained, the more excited his voice became. After the initial disappointment, I felt exuberant for him to have been awarded the contract. Suddenly I felt part of the adventure and in the middle of something new in my life. But I would not be meeting him before he left for Kuala Lumpur.

It was a little embarrassing to receive the call while driving with my grandchildren, for I had not shared this relationship with anyone. Now, confined on a car trip, I was vulnerable to the conversation and questions.

One of the girls, with a chuckle and smile, said, "Hey, Grandma, what's happening with this guy? You didn't tell us you have a new romance." In a teasing manner, they both chimed in with, "Tell us about him. What does he look like? Where did you meet him? What's his name? Where does he live? We're happy for you. Are you going to meet him here?" I quietly explained we had met about two months ago. I said, "It probably won't bloom into a romance. I am not going to meet him now as planned." Rather embarrassed, I said, "He's leaving the country, and that will be the end of it." They said, "Oh, Grandma, we are so sorry. Don't give up yet. Keep us posted on what happens." The conversation ended, and we went shopping.

I arrived at the airport the next day with sadness and disappointment. My luggage seemed heavier than usual. My energy was depleted. I felt lonely, angry and worried. As I walked past Jimmie's Grill, where we planned to meet, I felt envious of the travelers laughing and relaxing between flights.

It had been over two months of daily online communication and phone calls, but we still had not met. Thoughts quickly crossed my mind, "He is lying to me. He never intended to meet. How could he be so cruel? Why did he lead me on?" But then just as quickly and vividly I heard his last words, "Honey, we will be together in three months and have the rest of our lives." Like water rushing over the falls, his romantic words and mesmerizing voice washed over all my negative thoughts. I told myself, "All will work out. He is falling in love with me. Just a few months, and we will be together." I boarded the plane.

I arrived home that evening still feeling some disappointment but also some excitement for a future with Carl. He would be flying out the next day to Kuala Lumpur to start working on a contract that would benefit us for our future,

As I was unpacking from my flight, I received a phone call from him. I felt relieved that he wanted to talk with me before he was to leave the country the next morning. He said, "I am so sorry, Darling, that we didn't get to meet. But I know how wonderful you are just by our emails and phone calls. We know so much about each other, and it just seems so right." These were reassuring words, and I felt his excitement for the job. I told him, "Yes, I feel very connected in the relationship, although we haven't met. I feel your concern for me and desire to be with me. Will you let me know your address?" "Yes, Darling," he said, ""I will notify you of my housing location, cell phone, and when I will have internet access again. Remember, I am falling in love with you, and we will be together in no more than three months."

# Promises

Two days later, I received a phone call. Indeed, he had information for me on lodging. But with some frantic emotion he explained, "I am here with the supervisor and don't have the correct license to work this contract. The license I have is not accepted. I have some cash but not enough to pay for this license. Could you please wire me some cash? I will pay you back right away with interest." "No, Carl." I said, "I will not send money. You can wire your bank for money." His response, "I am trying, Darling, but they want me to draw money from the account here, in person, and I have no power of attorney to help."

"Carl," I questioned, " Why weren't you aware of this situation before traveling there?" He gave no firm answer. I asked again, and he continued to ignore my question. He kept pleading with me over and over again, "Honey, Darling, please send me the money so we can get on with our lives." He needed $9,000. I was shocked and gripped with emotion. I kept asking him, "Is this job legitimate, and why weren't you better prepared for this type of situation?" Sounding tearful and apologetic, he said, "I will get the money next week, and I will send you a copy of the contract. Don't worry. There will be plenty of money for us. Just help me now."

He emailed a picture of the contract and the license he needed. Soon he sent me pictures of the old apartment buildings, which he said were part of the demolition project. New complexes were being built to replace the old. It all seemed very legitimate. I could see in my mind the apartments he would be demolishing. My experience of having visited there gave me a sense of security that this really was true. I was embarking on an adventure with him, and it felt exciting.

This was the first of his many requests. I wired $9,000 to Kuala Lumpur Bank. The bank asked me questions when I wired the money. They said, "Do you know this person receiving the money? How long have you known him? Are you comfortable sending this much money? Does he live in the states or another country?" When they asked me these questions, I felt uncomfortable, but I also felt quite confident in my decision. Carl's emails had reassured me. He repeatedly said, "Honey, I am really fond of you. I can see us getting married. I will be gone only three months. We will be building our future."

With each transaction that followed, however, I felt increasingly nervous about sending money. It weighed on my mind that the bank would question my decisions. But, for over thirty years, I had been a client of the bank. Since I seemed competent and credible, they trusted my judgment and proceeded with each request. It became easier, not more complex. With smooth bank transactions and Carl's flattering romantic emails with promises for our future, I was scooped into his net!

# Romance

YouTube is phenomenal entertainment and easily accessible. Carl took full advantage of this medium. Celine Dion's performances in Las Vegas came with my emails almost daily. Her performance of "Power of Love" was among the most frequent along with his romantic poetry, telling me how much in love he was with me. From our conversations, he knew Lionel Richie and Kenny Rogers were among my favorite singers. Videos of Lionel Richie's "Endless Love," "Stuck on You," and Kenny Rogers singing "Lady" endeared him further to me. These predators are very careful to romance in an elegant, meaningful, classy approach, without offensive sexuality or porn. From very small bits of information, Carl knew how to expound just the right subjects with integrity, honesty, and class. Everyday phone calls and emails contained music and endearing comments.

The romance deepened quite soon, with constant phoning and emails. One day I asked him, "You are phoning so often from Malaysia. What is your phone bill? How can you afford this and still ask me for money?" He would always respond with, "I have a good phone and unlimited time. Don't worry, Honey, we will always be in touch. I will make sure I can pay for our calls."

Unknowingly, more requests for money were soon to follow. Trust was building. His captivating voice and charm intensified my belief that we would have a future together. He soothed my long workdays with always having a message in the evening waiting for me. Either I had a phone call or an email. Often, he said, " I am your man. I want to be your husband." My response at times was guarded. Once I told him, "Carl, I am not sure about making such definite plans so soon. We have not met. There is plenty of time when you finish the job. "I was rather uncomfortable with this sort of conversation. In the past, I didn't make rash decisions and long-term commitments. But still I kept in touch. He would say, "We have a lasting love. I know we do. Please, please don't doubt me." Music videos arrived more frequently. All were designed to move our relationship forward through love songs, original poetry, scenes of romantic vacation spots, and love notes accompanied with flowers. He started elevating his emotions about getting the job completed sooner so he could return to "my love." Of course, all of it was leading to another request. Early one morning, I received a phone call from him. Upon answering, I detected the urgency in his voice along with his romancing of "Did you sleep well, Sweetheart?" Not waiting for an answer, he plunged into detail saying, "I know it is early, Darling, but I have something very exciting to talk about. I know you will be excited as well. Listen . . . Listen . . . Are you awake and listening?"

"Yes, Carl, I am listening," I said. "But calm down and explain what is happening." Still with much emotion, he said, "Listen, my darling, I want to get this job completed much sooner. They have so little machinery. It is taking forever! I don't want to be gone much longer from you." His voice was raised in pitch. It sounded like he was almost crying. Then in a burst of excitement, he said, "I have the solution. They told me I could rent more machinery, and the job would be completed sooner." Again, in his pleading voice, he said, "I know we want to be together really soon. I can cut a month off the time here if I rent more machinery. "

Alarmed about hearing of yet another conflict, I very emphatically said, "What is needed, Carl? Contact your supervisor and tell them what you want. Take care of it. I have no idea why you have to consult me." After a rather long pause, he responded saying, "We are in this together, Darling. I will need money to rent machinery. It is for us. I will be home a month sooner. Don't you understand?"

"UNDERSTAND!" I said, "YOU do not understand. Why doesn't the contractor help you? If you want to rent machinery, pay for it. I have no more money to give you." Pleading, he said, "You know I don't have enough money with me and no way to get it from my bank. I promise I will pay you back with interest. In the end, you will have more than you give me. We are a team. It will be wonderful to be together. I will need $20,000." Again, I said, "NO. The answer is no." I don't recall what happened in this conversation that made me change my mind. I do remember he pleaded for an extra amount of cash to help with his living expenses. Before the phone conversation was over, I told him I would send $25,000 to rent machinery and help with cash flow to the end of the job.

The thought of him being a scam artist never entered my mind, even at this point. Again, my gut aches, nausea hits, and a chill comes over me even seven years later as I share this journey. I was not a person who had spent much time researching about things on the internet. Consequently, I was not aware of this "romance" being a scam. Now, after nearly three months into this so-called relationship, I had not shared it with anyone. Who would believe I would do such a thing? No one would understand like I thought I did! I was immersed in an adventure that was to go nowhere but down.

# Beneficiary

It has now been a month since Carl has arrived in Malaysia. The romantic music videos, kind words, and news of my daily activities took up much of the conversation. In a depressed mood, he often shared about his difficult, long workdays. He said, "The neighborhood I walk through is so dangerous. I fear for my life, Darling. I want to move from this hotel. I need a different area closer to work."

Again, I could relate to this scene. I had visited Kuala Lumpur. I recall the dark streets and alleys. He complained about the cost of food and how little he was getting paid on the contract until it was completed. Casually he remarked, "My money is running out." Now his emails read, "I hope my money lasts until my contract payment is paid. Some days I worry so much about not seeing you again. I eat very little. I miss you so much. I want to finish this job for our future."

At this point, I remember thinking, "This is not true. I am caught up in something and don't know where to go. I am trapped, but yet I want to stay in touch with him. How can he be having so much trouble? I think he is going to ask for more money." I became restless and didn't sleep well. I worried about all the money that I had already sent him.

The next request was for more cash, in spite of the additional money I had sent along with the fee for the machinery rental. Also, his contract money was being held up due to his expired travel documents. He would go to jail if $50,000 wasn't paid before his check was issued.

In addition--he wanted me to become the beneficiary of his contract money. The conversation was saturated with romantic promises. He was a master at building trust, and at the same time, requesting money.

Carl said he would need a lawyer to confirm the beneficiary document and to make all details legal. I questioned him in these discussions. By now I was asking MYSELF many questions. I had already wired him money twice. I wanted assurance from him that the money would be returned if something were to happen to him. The Certificate of Beneficiary sounded like a good idea. With his romantic words, our future together and the "legal" document to give me security, he had not missed a trick. I WAS OUT OF TOUCH WITH REALITY.

Carl emailed the Malaysian lawyer's information to me. I questioned it for two or three days. Doubts entered my mind. I emailed the lawyer to check his authenticity. He responded with the following email. With some incorrect usages of our English language, it was somewhat disturbing to me. But again, I told myself it was because he was Malaysian. English was not his first language.

> Madam, Carole,
>
> Firstly, I want you to know that everything about Carl Williams is legit and real. He's a nice and gentleman. I knew about the beneficiary. He told me that you are his wife and wanted you to be his beneficiary. I did advise him if he trusted you and he said YES, he do and you are all he has so, I advised him to go ahead with the beneficiary. I also signed at the place of submission of the documents to make everything go fine. So, Mrs. Carole, there is nothing to worry about the beneficiary issue.
>
> I am the person that will be contacting you if necessary. The immigration authorities are holding his paycheck for expired travel documents. The penalty fee is $50,000. He is presently working off the penalty with hard work instead

of jail. I have been doing my job as lawyer to help him and assure him the government is not taking advantage of him. Fees are imposed on noncitizen contractors so there may be additional fees for his noncitizen situation also. But for now, this is the situation.

You may contact me for any of your questions.

OHAN ASSOCIATES
Advocates & Solicitors
Malaysia
Tel: +60-169-681-085
Email: barristerchan@lawyer.com

Adequate information was shared in the email to convince me it was all legitimate. I wired $58,000 to cover expired documents and living expenses. Carl sent me a copy of the Certificate of Beneficiary. It appeared legitimate, just as the previous documents he sent. He called this an "investment in our future." I now had wired the Bank of Malaysia three different times without any difficulty. Carl responded each time that he had received the money. I had sent $92,000. It was not over. I was truly invested in our relationship. In hindsight, how ridiculous it was to think I would be his beneficiary!

I now had the beneficiary document and felt Carl would be finishing the job soon. We continued to communicate by phone and email from Kuala Lumpur. His romantic videos and poetry were more powerful with each email. I questioned where he was getting this poetry. He said, "I often wrote poetry for my wife. I loved her very much, and she really enjoyed when I wrote her poems and read them aloud to her. I am so glad you like it, too." Interest of writing was another thing we had in common. It took only tidbits of information in my profile for him to wiggle into the web of romance with me.

We were counting the weeks until his return to the states. He detailed all the things we would do upon his return. I fantasized traveling to Germany with him to the areas I loved and was eager to revisit. Our shared ancestry felt very exciting to me. He was from Berlin; my ancestors were from near Heidelberg. Even though we were long distance, I felt we were building a relationship. Many of our interests were fitting together.

He knew just how to play the drums to the beat of my desires. He would often say during our phone conversations, "These dollars I am earning now will bring a wonderful life for us. I am eager to start a life together."

In early January, I received a call in his pleading voice, "I need more money to complete the job early. It is very important that I do so. I am running out of money for the hotel. I am so eager to see you. I am so fond of you." He pleaded with me in a teary emotional manner, "There is just not enough machinery and labor to get the job done in a reasonable time." He said, "Renting more machinery and hiring more labor will get me back to you, my lovely lady." Everyday living expenses were more than he had anticipated. He complained that he was paid halfway through the contracted time with just half the salary and was running out of money. Over and over he said, "Taxes, Taxes. I have to pay taxes before I leave the country. They won't let me leave, and I won't have all my paycheck yet. I need $150,000. Please, Please, send it to me. They will not let me leave unless I pay it."

There was a different twist to this now. He asked me to listen carefully to where I should send it. He asked that I wire the money to Bank of America in Sacramento, California. It would go to a specific account, ABL, addressed to a specific person. He was very convincing that this was because he didn't want me to be questioned about sending money again. He said, "If you send it from a different bank, it will be safer. It won't raise questions about me the way it might if you sent again from the same bank and to the same person in Malaysia." He explained he would be able to receive it through this named addressee of the account. He would provide that information to me when I was ready to wire the money.

Sending the money to a new location sounded logical to me. I asked several times, "What does ABL stand for?" He said, "Oh, it is a name of the account of my friend, and he will see that I get the money. He lives in Sacramento, California." At that time, I was not searching the internet, clarifying various locations of businesses. Searching things out on the computer was not my forte. The fact that it was going to a bank seemed legitimate.

My major concern was where would I come up with $150,000? My investments were drained as well as my savings. I had advanced money on my credit cards as well. I told him I had no more money. I absolutely would not send more. I was extremely nervous.

He had ideas for me. Did I have a car? Was it paid for? How much could I draw on a credit card? Did I have any more investments? With his pleading and his romantic overtures on the phone and email, he once again reached my heart.

I recall so vividly where I was when he called. Standing in the grocery store parking lot, I answered my cell. "Have you made arrangements, Darling? You know I will pay you back with interest. Don't worry, my Sweet, all will be ok," his voice trailed off. All I could feel and hear was my pounding heart. I said, "Yes, Carl, I am on my way to take care of it." I was feeling desperation about my money being returned with interest. Doubt was starting to creep into my mind. I seemed to repeat his words of, "All will be ok." As I relive this moment and write, it seems unbelievable that I felt the need to send money for our future.

My major concern was where would I come up with $150,000? I was extremely nervous. What had I done? I was not sleeping at night. He would be home soon and pay me back with interest. Those were my comforting words. How could I quit now? I would never get my money back. I drew cash against my car and withdrew cash from credit cards. I rationalized he would be home soon and pay me the money with interest. I wired money once again.

The days passed, and I felt excitement now that he was nearing completion of the contract. I counted the days for him to fly into Arizona. I felt we were in the home stretch.

Soon there was another request. He needed money for the airline ticket with Delta Airlines and tax to exit the country. He said, "They were to take money out of my earnings for tax, but they are not going to pay my earnings up front. It will be deposited in my bank in Washington. I cannot leave the country until I pay it. I have no money for my ticket to come and see you, my love."

I felt angry, fearful, frustrated, tearful, and worried that I had been betrayed. How would I handle this? Over and over, I asked myself, "Could this really be true? I called him and said, "I cannot do this. I will not send more money. Not even to fly you here. I feel betrayed. You are lying to me. You have lied to me this entire time." It felt good to be angry and yell. But soon I felt I would lose everything if I turned him away. He had such a powerful hold on me. I was convinced that he would pay me back the money. If I had only confided in someone along the way, maybe they would have steered me away from this disaster.

Three days went by and I tried to ignore his romantic calls and pleading. Finally, I thought one more time, and he will be here. I will buy the plane ticket and get him here. He will have to find the money for the tax.

Again, he wanted the money wired to "ABL" at the Bank of America in Sacramento, California. I asked for details on the flight. I pleaded with him now, "Please send me the following information: what day, time, flight number, and a detailed flight itinerary." He emailed all that information to me, along with the price. With this solid information, I decided to think it through one more day. I called the airline. Yes, these were the exact details available. He must be telling me the truth. I decided not to send the tax money. But when I told him this, he pleaded and pleaded, saying they would not let him out of the country unless he paid the salary tax.

It's like eating popcorn, and you can't stop at one kernel. But it's thousands of dollars not popcorn! The heart does not listen to the mind. They are totally disconnected. A logical voice in my head said, "Do not send more money." My trusting personality and heart told me to send it, and he will be home soon to pay it back with interest. Not only had I been hooked, but I was being reeled in. I was caught in a net securely ready to be tossed ashore.

I wired more money. I was certain he would be coming on that Delta flight. As I wired $128,800 to the Sacramento bank, I promised myself I would send no more. My money was depleted, and I was worried!!

It was now January. The day Carl would arrive at Sky Harbor. I received a phone call. Eagerly I answered, hoping he was well on his way and perhaps at one of the airports making a change. His pleading voice said, "I am ready to board Delta in Kula Lumpur, and the authorities will not let me go. I am being detained by security." My heart sank. It not only sank, but it pounded fast and heavy. My intuition told me I had been had! I wasn't crying now. I was so angry I could hardly breath. I didn't say anything. I could hear voices in the background, but I was unable to understand anyone. Finally, he said, "Darling, are you there? I need your help. The authorities have me held here. I will go to jail if I don't pay the immigration fee to leave the country." I responded with calmness now, for I immediately knew I had to get all the information possible to report him. My adrenaline kicked in, and I would have strangled him if he had been near.

Quietly and calmly I asked, "Carl, you have a plane ticket, the salary tax is paid, what more do you need?" He said, "Oh, Honey, if you could just quickly wire me $5000 more, I can be on my way home to you. This is terrible here. The authorities are treating me horribly."

He had previously emailed me a copy of the Delta Airline ticket. I had the flight information. But my gut immediately told me it had to be a fake ticket, just like all the rest of the documents he so carefully provided. This January morning, it all unfolded before me. Finally, I listened to my intuition. No honest person would continue asking for thousands of dollars.

I told him, "No, there will be no more cash sent. You are a criminal. You have lied, been deceitful, and taken all my money. I will be calling the authorities here and reporting you." Of course, he started to plead. I disconnected the call.

It was over. I was scammed. I hardly knew what scammed meant in the online dating world. I never felt I was a naive woman. But this left me feeling totally stupid, embarrassed, and angry.

# I've Been Scammed

○ ○ ○

*Sunday Morning, January 2013*

I HAVE BEEN SCAMMED! It was a bright, sunny January morning in Arizona. My heart had hit rock bottom, pounding with fear, guilt, anger, embarrassment, nausea, and overall weakness encasing my body. The reality had hit that Carl would not be arriving at the airport today or ever. His desperate phone call needing MORE money for clearance at the Malaysian customs or go to jail was a jolt to my body that is still present in my gut, even as I write today, seven years later. Over three short months of wiring thousands of dollars to him, it was shockingly clear to me I was in deep trouble.

The airline confirmation arrived in his email the day before, thanking me for the airline fare I wired to him. FAKE DOCUMENTS. Light bulbs lit up all over my brain like firecrackers. Where had my mind been all this time? Shaking with disbelief, I called Delta Airlines. The woman who answered was kind, but said, "Madam, there is a flight leaving Malaysia at that time, but we do not have a passenger by the name of Carl Williams holding a ticket." In shock, I kept questioning her over and over, with tears starting to stream down my face, I sobbed, "Are you absolutely sure there is not a Carl Williams reservation? I have a copy of his reservation in my hand." Finally, she said, "Madam, I know this is upsetting, but please believe me, I have the passenger list in front of me and there is not a passenger with a ticket by that name. I am sorry." I had to believe her. I have traveled enough to know she had to have been looking at the list.

At that moment, I hated this man with a passion. How could anyone do that to me? Never had I betrayed anyone in my life. What had I done? How could I be so stupid? Who would believe I did this? I wanted to hide. Hate and anger stayed with me a very long time as well as many more feelings I was about to experience.

Carl had told me he was required to register at the Malaysian Embassy upon arrival in Kuala Lumpur. Still in disbelief, I called the embassy. I was able to speak with a clerk and asked, "Can you please check the name of a USA citizen who arrived in your country on a work permit? I need to know if he is there. His name is Carl Williams." The clerk said, "I can check for you, but it is highly unlikely he is here. Just a moment." Upon his return to the phone he asked, "Did you meet this gentleman through a dating agency?" I replied, "Yes, but he came there to work on a contract." He kindly, but rather reluctantly replied, "I have checked for you, and there is no one registered by that name. Regretfully, I believe you may be another victim of the ongoing ring of criminals financially scamming single women for thousands of dollars. Good luck, Lady. It happens a lot."

My heart dropped to my toes. My hands were shaking. I walked the floor. Stupid! Stupid! Stupid! How could a person with any brains at all do this? I thought I was an intelligent, professional woman with common sense. Mortified and in shock, I sat a moment, then walked the floor, then sat another few minutes, then walked the floor. There was no solution coming to my mind. I just couldn't process this. Who should I call? Who should I go to for advice? What advise was there to get? I had sent thousands of dollars to this scum of the earth in just three short months. Who would ever believe that an intelligent woman could empty her bank account to someone she has never met? Only someone who had experienced a nightmare like this would believe it, and I certainly didn't know anyone as stupid as me at this point. The tears started as I sat and tried to think of someone who would understand and help me. After several moments of crying and feeling sorry for myself, anger set in. Now I was ready to go after this horrible son of a bitch. One moment I was angry, and then devastation set in. There had to be someone to call.

The day before I was expecting Carl to arrive, I went to the grocery store for last minute items. Making sure not to forget anything, I had a list in hand of special foods he said he liked. Having waited so long, I wanted things to be as perfect as possible.

As I was getting out of my car in the grocery store parking lot, Sherry was parked beside me. Sherry and I had played golf together for several seasons. We had shared many stories on the nineteenth hole about not having companions, about having companions but not having any fun, about decisions to just forget dating, and about thoughts like, "Oh Dear Lord, some gals are luckier than others." We had each other's back always.

As I hurriedly grabbed my purse and slammed the car door, I called, "Hey, Sherry." She came over and said, "WOW, you look excited, what's happening?" I started rambling away saying, "I have some great news to tell you. I have been involved in online dating. I met a guy named Carl. He is arriving tomorrow to meet in person for the first time." With a big smile, Sherry said, "WOW, I didn't know you found someone online. Cool, is he a good catch?" I leaned over and quietly said, "Oh, my gosh, is he ever. We have been emailing and calling each other for three months. He has wired flowers and cards and really seems sincere. He is finally coming to see me. He's pretty handsome, dances, wants to travel, has a German background. Oh, I am really excited. Honestly, Sherry, we seem to be so well matched. I barely told him a thing about me, and he has so many of the same interests. This online dating seems like it might be the answer." I told her, "He went to Malaysia on a contract to increase his retirement for us. She questioned, "Why would he do that? You haven't met him yet?" "No," I said, "but he is really eager to see me, and from all his emails and phone calls, I believe it is for real and it is going to work out for a future together." She didn't question the circumstances anymore and was really happy I found someone. We were two senior women in the grocery store, chatting away like teenagers again. We decided love and companionship was what we all needed at any age. I assured her I would share my excitement of how it would unfold.

Tomorrow he would arrive, and I would know if there was real attraction. I wasn't worried. He would be paying back the money, with interest, that I had sent him. But in my heart, I was feeling the real thing. Of course, I had not shared with Sherry the fact I had sent him thousands of dollars over the three months. I was confident no one but he and I would know. Oh, my dear God, what a fool I was.

Who would I call for help since so few of my friends knew I was dating online? I decided to call Sherry.

I found my cell phone and nervously picked it up. Tears flooded my eyes. I could hardly read the numbers to dial. As the phone was ringing, I asked myself, "How stupid would she think I am? Could I even tell her I gave money to him?" She answered and I started sobbing, barely able to speak. "Sherry," I said, "A terrible thing has happened, and I need you to come over right away. Can you do that?" She said, "Yes, I will be there in just a few minutes. What is happening?" I continued crying and could only say, "I have been stupid, Carl is not a real person." I ended the call. She arrived in just a few minutes. As she came in the door, she hugged me and said, "I am here to help you. Just tell me what happened, and together we will do what we need to do."

Slowly, I regained control of my emotions. I told her, "Carl swindled me out of thousands of dollars. He is a fake person. He lied to me. I believed him for several months. I am so stupid." Keeping calm, Sherry assured me, "We will file a report. You are not stupid, Carole. He has probably conned many other unfortunate women. I'll stay here with you. I will help you call the police. You know you have my support." She gave me another big hug and said, "Let's get this information together. This is a huge crime. We'll call the police, and you can give them all the information to get it started so that they can try and track down this con artist. . . and while we work on it, we need to pour a glass of wine."

She took two wine glasses from the cupboard. As she poured the

Merlot, my thoughts traveled everywhere. I took a deep breath, a sip of wine, and vowed, "I will rally above this." I then dialed the police. Sherry stood by with moral support.

Shaking and teary, I gave my name to the police department and then said, "I want to file charges of fraud." The response was, "We will need to come to your address to file the complaint. Could you give us your address? We will come right away." At that moment, I realized I couldn't remember my own address. I said, "I don't remember. I am in total shock. What is it, Sherry?" Sherry came to my rescue and read it to them.

In just a few minutes, a police car drove up to my house. It was the first time a police officer had ever come to my home. It brought an instant flash of memories when police officers came to serve eviction notices to my parents for nonpayment of rent. When that happened during my high school years, I felt humiliated. Those visits always meant we had to move again.

Humiliation consumed me now. I tried to bring my focus back to the present as the female officer walked to the door of my home. I froze where I stood. Sherry answered the doorbell.

With a cordial greeting the officer introduced herself, "Hello, I am Officer Marilyn Stellworth." She appeared to be in her mid-forties, tall, wearing her uniform proudly and with confidence. Her dark hair tucked under her cap gave her a professional appearance. She greeted us with a warm smile. Slowly I found the words to say, "This is Sherry, my friend. I am in shock but will try to give you information." The officer said, "Please take your time. We can gather information from your notes that are here. I see you have papers on the table. Are they notes for me? If you have statements of his requests for money, dates and emails, that is a good start." She continued to say, "I am so very sorry for this horrific loss and what you are experiencing. We will file the statement. You will most likely want to retain a lawyer and proceed with his advice. There are various ways of proceeding after you gather all your information." She added, "I am very pleased you are filing a charge. Many people under these circumstances will not come forward to acknowledge being conned. It is an extremely difficult situation." I was surprised and said, "Are you telling me there are many others who have the same experience?" She said, "Oh, yes, thousands of women and men are conned online, but hundreds and thousands do not report it. Calling to report the fraud is the first step. But if not reported, nothing can proceed toward charges. Therefore, thousands of cases exist, and nothing can be done about them. You are very brave to come forward, and we thank you for doing so." Hearing this from her consoled me in a small way. But I totally understood why thousands do not come forward and admit this feeling of anger, stupidity, shame, and guilt. It was devastating.

Somehow, under all this duress, I provided what was needed and signed the papers. The officer emphasized that my file would be available for future use in charges that could be filed. She said, "Please continue your investigation of this horrific crime and contact me for any assistance you may need." As she left, I felt a bit of relief, but I was totally confused as to what I would do next.

Between tears, vomiting, and overall devastation, I managed to make a list of action items for the next day. Sherry offered her help and support and then went home when I assured her that I would be ok. I made a pot of tea and started going over my list. At the very top, I wrote that I needed to contact a lawyer. From there, I could perhaps get additional guidance. I also knew that I needed to gather the proof of the money I wired to him and list the dates of the emails he sent asking for money along with the promises he made. All of this was terribly painful to think about and organize.

It was not on my list to notify my family. I felt they would be the last ones to tell. I was quite sure I would figure this out and move on with my life so they would not need to know. Shock and embarrassment were the major reasons why I made this decision. I went to bed but slept very little. Most of the night, I was up making toast with peanut butter and drinking hot tea. I would vomit, and then make more tea, eat toast, and vomit. It was as if it all would go away if I ate and drank tea. I felt crazy, tearful, hungry, and sick. I just wanted to leave the world and hide somewhere.

Since moving to Arizona, I had never used a lawyer's services. Who would I call to handle such a huge dilemma? I personally knew only one criminal lawyer in Arizona. She was a ballroom dancing friend. Although I had not shared my online dating experience with her, I felt now, in this crisis, I could share in confidence my serious situation. Patty would have empathy, and she would help in any way possible. If she was not able to take my case, I knew she could refer me to someone who had the legal experience I needed. I had confidence in her.

Morning arrived, and I knew I had to call Patty. My heart throbbed with anxiety as I dialed her cell. "Hello, Patty. This is Carole. Do you have a few moments to visit?" "Yes, of course," she said. "What's going on? Are you going dancing tonight?" "No, Patty," I responded nervously. "I have some terrible news, and I need your help. I know I can share with you in confidence. I need a lawyer, and if it is not in your interest of law, I would like your recommendation. If you have any suggestions, I would really appreciate your help." Her response was quick and to the point. "Carole, tell me briefly, are you ok? Are you injured? What has happened?" I told her what happened. She said, " It will be a long investigation. You will need a lawyer to deal with frauds and con artists, which is not what I handle. You will also most likely need a private investigator." Then she said, "It will be a hard battle, one you should fight, but you need to realize there may be little or no restitution." Speaking with sincere concern, she said, "You definitely need a real sleuth and an outstanding lawyer. I can refer you to both. I will explain to them what has happened and let them know you are my friend." She gave me their contact information, and I was ready to move forward. Patty was a professional, and she had my back. She was well aware of the frauds existing all over the world. If only I had shared my online dating with her before I sent any money.

# The Private Investigator

○  ○  ○

It was mid-morning, and I was pacing the floor for what seemed like hours. The private investigator was arriving this morning. I dreaded the interview that would expose my stupidity once again.

Patty had been in criminal law for many years. She was connected and referred me to Paul Rubin. His references described him as analytical, with considerable IT experience, and a keen eye for investigating fraud cases. She assured me he would be kind and understanding about my situation. I was thinking up all kinds of excuses to defend myself. I was sure he would ask, "Why would an intelligent person let this happen?" I wondered how to explain to a complete stranger how I was pulled in so easily?

A car pulled up in front of my house. Paul Rubin was a wiry, energetic, well-dressed man who walked quickly like a man on a mission. Thoughts raced through my mind. I was afraid he would fire questions at me so fast I wouldn't be able to answer. Was I a fool for hiring him only to discover funds couldn't be recovered? My bank account was empty. I was scared and filled with shame. I was nervous, very emotional and suffering from shock. I needed someone I could totally rely on for suggestions and answers. I felt vulnerable and alone, with no idea how to go forward. I felt weak and helpless like someone being swallowed by quicksand.

Paul shook my hand warmly and explained the interview would be difficult. He was extremely interested in the case, and he pored over the paperwork for hours day after day. He searched all the emails we sent back and forth for clues that might lead to Carl's location. Paul was certain "Carl" was a ring of criminals--not one lone man who committed this crime against me and he was committed to catching them trying to ease the pain of my financial loss.

There were mounds of papers waiting to be thoroughly searched stacked on my dining room table. I gathered piles of emails, hard copies, and fake documents proving he asked for money using the excuse that he needed it for various jobs and licenses. Paul searched my computer to discover where the criminal(s) were located. His biggest concern would be tracking anyone outside of the USA. I had received a reply from the Malaysian Embassy that this was a common incident. Within a day, Paul discovered Carl was part of a Nigerian online dating scam.

Within the first forty-eight hours of the investigation, Paul kept asking, "Have you notified your kids?" I kept telling him, "No, I can't tell them. What would they think of their mom doing such a horrible, stupid thing?" Initially I thought, "It really is not your concern if I notify my kids." Later, after he became a daily visitor to my home diligently searching for any clues, I realized he had been through this before. He knew how important it was to have family there for support and guidance.

Certainly, there was no evidence that there would ever be restitution. But Paul's determination to uncover something that would lead us to some results kept me hopeful. My body was numb with the emotional pain of seeing all the documents. There were several hundred emails of lies. As I read them again, the false promises he made cut through my body like knives ripping open an animal and hate rose up inside of me.

Paul and I worked closely every day that week. I learned his wife was facing serious neurosurgery soon. Coincidentally my son was scheduled for serious brain surgery to remove a tumor. We shared our common concerns for our loved ones of serious impairment or death. My family was consumed with prayers dedicated to my son's recovery. How could I share this terrible news with them at this critical time in his life? How would we all cope with my son's medical crisis and this horrible trauma in my life at the same time? I was consumed by guilt, shame, and worry. I wasn't the mom rescuing my family. Instead, my family needed to rescue me. We were all making plans to fly out of state to be together, but I was creating this horrific drama while my son's life was in danger.

Finally, I knew I had to call my children. They were all grown up, all married with families of their own. I hoped they could cope with this other upsetting news. I called my daughters first, one at a time, and then my son. I said, "This is your mom. I have some tragic news to share. I am not injured physically, but I am broken emotionally and financially. I am sorry to say that my lonely heart took over my mind, and, consequently, I have been scammed. I have lost thousands of dollars. I will work through it, but you need to know what is happening. I want you to know that sharing this humiliating situation with you is one of the hardest things I have ever done. I know you love me. I need your moral support as I build my life again." They all responded the same way. "Mom, we didn't know you were so lonesome. We are so sorry. What can we do?" My children expressed their shock and anger at the perpetrator. I was seventy-six years old. Years had passed since my divorce. My family was scattered throughout four different states. We were all in contact and shared our activities. We were supportive of each other, but miles have a way of limiting visits. It was easy to shield my family from my loneliness. Unfortunately, a professional criminal found my lonely heart and knew how to reach out and take advantage of that void.

# Paralyzed

I was paralyzed with fear and anger. My mind could not seem to process anything, and I was unable to eat. I could not sort out this financial chaos on my own.

Within a few days of calling my family, my daughters flew to my home to be with me. Adding to what seemed to be insurmountable stress, my son, awaiting surgery, was now forced to deal with details of his mother's tragedy as well. He was unable to travel at that time, but when my daughters arrived, we hugged and cried over and over again. It felt heart wrenching to receive this love and compassion from them. I felt blessed and relieved to have them with me. I knew their business and organizational abilities were going to be very useful to me at this time. They both said, "Mom, we got this. We will put it together and get you back on your feet."

I showed them the dining room table covered with mounds of papers, and the computer inbox full of this criminal's promises, lies, and false words of love. My daughters worked night and day for a week combing over documents with notes and ledgers. I made sure there were always snacks on the table while they assessed bank statements and wired money receipts. They developed a system to file all this information onto painstakingly created spreadsheets itemizing my losses. Sadly, I was of no assistance to them. I couldn't eat, sleep, or think about anything except the guilt and financial loss. When the girls asked for more information, I numbly went about collecting what I could pull up on files of records or receipts. At that time, total shock had set in. I could only recall what was documented on paper.

# Events in Motion

The mortgage on my house was due. My car, once debt free, required payments now because of the money I borrowed against it, along with payments I needed to make on money I borrowed on my credit cards. Thousands of dollars, once secure in investments, were gone. Income budgeted for my expenses from those investments was no longer available. Now my only income was Social Security and a small pension. It wasn't enough to continue living in my current home. With this loss of income and huge debt, it seemed very likely that I would lose both my home and my car.

How could a professionally educated woman with a reputation for stability and common sense appear to have lost all reason? Every time I thought like this, I started vomiting and shaking with chills. I could not imagine how to move forward. My family worked for hours trying to put a plan together for my future. It seemed hopeless to me.

We were fortunate to schedule an appointment with a lawyer while my daughters were still visiting. Once again, I turned to Patty for the referral, and once again, I dreaded telling another professional my horrible story. No doubt I would appear to be a very naive, ignorant woman.

I was petrified and vomited again before we drove to the city to meet with him. I prayed I would not appear too foolish. Previous memories of lawyers for my divorce flooded my mind. All I could think of was the divorce settlement, papers to sign, disagreements, low self-esteem, financial loss, and my overall pain dealing with a change of lifestyle. The thoughts of returning to the rigid atmosphere of a law office was upsetting.

We loaded the files of my daughters' well-documented paperwork into the car. I could never have done it myself. As I reflect on that moment, I marvel at the work and support they gave me. The hour-long drive to the office felt like an eternity. We were greeted by office staff and seated in a conference room. My heart pounded like horse hooves on pavement. My daughters kept reassuring me that this lawyer would help us. I thought the long conference table and chairs were very intimidating. I pictured myself in a courtroom, about to be sentenced for a crime. Shame weighed heavily on me. I was humiliated being duped by a con artist. The SOB was smarter than me and probably felt no guilt nor would he be sentenced! I couldn't think of anything positive and my mind raced a thousand pathways none of them connected. All I could feel was the silence of a courtroom waiting for the judge to enter.

Soon a tall, distinguished gentleman came into the courtroom with a calm energy that flooded over me and now I felt like I was in a library with a silence that brought me peace. It was a soothing light showering down over me like liquid silver. It was calming and pleasantly energizing. I could sense my daughters relaxing. My breathing slowed. I felt the walls of this library ooze with knowledge and God's peace was present. I knew at that moment, if anyone could offer advice and support in this financial crisis, it would be this man. He introduced himself as Stan Gregory. He had a soft but distinct voice and gentle mannerisms.

My daughters presented the files they had so painstakingly prepared. The spreadsheets documented the financial consequences I faced because of the scam. Mr. Gregory could review all the wired money transactions, including penalties for withdrawals from investments, the advances on credit cards, the mortgage payments, the lien on my car that was paid off at one point, and many other expenses, too many to detail here.

Mr. Gregory's face looked dazed by it all. I wondered what he was thinking. His gentle, calm voice, full of compassion, touched me deeply. He asked several questions, which brought up more concerns. Mr. Gregory asked, "Are charges being filed on this predator? Is the case being investigated? Who is working on it? Do they give you any hope of restitution?" I kept waiting for him to ask me, "How could you do such a terrible thing?" Thankfully, he was kind enough not to ask that question and for that, I was extremely grateful.

○   ○   ○

I spent a considerable amount of time with my lawyer discussing the pros and cons of filing for bankruptcy. He asked me, "How will you continue mortgage payments on your home? How will you pay credit card debt? What is your guaranteed income? Do you have any savings left? Can you pay your health insurance? What about auto maintenance, payment and insurance? After I answered these questions and reconciled all my accounts, I decided against filing for bankruptcy. Eventually, I decided the best thing to do was to sell my home and work as many hours as possible for income and health insurance. I had to maintain a car for work, and I would pay off debt as soon as possible.

While my daughters were still with me, I let go of my car. I will never forget seeing my precious vehicle loaded on to a flatbed tow truck and hauled away for auction. My credit rating was at rock bottom, but I still needed a car to keep my job. Before my daughters returned home, we shopped for a cheaper car. It turned out that leasing a vehicle was the best option, and I still needed additional help from my family to meet other living expenses.

After my family returned to their own homes, despair, loneliness, guilt, and overall stupidity consumed me. I tried to console myself by acknowledging what I was thankful for, but it felt exhausting to maintain a positive attitude each day. I still had my job as sales manager for the design company. I also designed ballroom dresses and traveled around the country selling and designing gowns at ballroom dance competitions. I could work and try to recover some of my loss. Over the years, I was known for being a professional, intelligent, hard-working, energetic person. WOW. Where was that woman who was so successful? I wondered how I could have done such a STUPID thing!

# How Could I Do Something That Stupid?

O O O

When I thought about how I could do something so stupid and what made me so vulnerable to this scam, I realized how dangerous a lonely heart could be to a woman or a man. Grief over Jake's death was long and painful. It kept me in a state of loneliness for two to three years. I was very familiar with the stages of grief (denial, anger, bargaining, depression, and acceptance) because of the work I did as an oncology nurse. However, it was much different assisting others through the process or teaching nursing students about the stages versus going through it myself. At times it was indescribably painful. Coping by myself and starting a new life again was no small challenge. Just when I thought I was moving ahead one step, I would fall back two, which is so often what happens. Working through the grieving process and having no companionship created a cave of depression.

Since I was unable to pay my mortgage, I had to move to a rental home. I started looking right away, knowing I would only have a few months before I would have to move. For the time being, my home furnishings remained in my possession. Moving to a rental home was a dark tragedy on my list of necessary changes. I had invested thousands of dollars into my home, and I had decorated it with love. In truth, I could live with minimal material belongings, but my heart and soul were fragile. I felt broken into thousands of ugly pieces, certainly not like a colorful urn that had been shattered. It felt more like a demolition with hunks of stone and various structures strewn around in no particular order. Instead of having beauty in my life, everything felt dirty and out of place. Shame does not reveal beauty, only ugliness. I knew I had much to be thankful for. My family did not abandon me. I had good physical health. I had a job. I could start over. But I needed to emotionally heal and regain my faith. It was still very difficult in these dark hours to recognize my blessings.

o o o

It was February 2013, six weeks after the tragic Sunday morning phone call from Carl, when he told me he would not be coming to see me. The weeks had passed with agonizing fatigue and worry trying to put my life back together. The date came to travel to the Midwest for my son's surgery.

Recently widowed, Doug was supported by the rest of our family with his children, siblings, and parents. His team of doctors were exceptional, having pioneered this procedure. Doug's friend, a physician standing by, also welcomed and supported us. It was a cold February day in Chicago. The icy wind screamed through the large hospital windows. We wanted to hear positive words from the physician as we rallied together for the long awaited outcome. The entire family was feeling anxious about this medical procedure. For me, the penetrating cold of Chicago in February added to the deep shame I felt from being scammed. However, I kept my prayers focused on a successful outcome for my son's surgery. After many hours spent in the surgical waiting room, we had good news. The doctor reported, "We were able to remove the tumor successfully, and it was not cancer." What a relief! The waiting was over. My son could start his recovery.

During that time at the hospital, my brother passed away suddenly. Although I dearly wanted to be in two places at once, I knew I had to stay at the hospital with my son. Fortunately, my brother's family understood my situation and offered me tremendous support. It felt extremely traumatic to lose my brother and not be able to attend his memorial service and spend time with his family. My brother and I had been good pals all our life. During my childhood, when I had hardly any parental support, I definitely relied on my big brother. His death and my son's surgery put me on an emotional rollercoaster of grief for my brother and joy for my son.

A significant amount of depression accompanied these waves of emotion. When I thought of Carl's broken promises, I felt very angry and hurt. He clearly told me that he would be with me in February to support me through this trauma. He said he wanted to be part of my family. I asked myself, "How could I have been so blind to think he would be there for me? I totally believed his romantic words, his seductive voice, the beautiful music and videos, and all of his promises. How could anyone be so cruel and thoughtless to run this type of scam?

When my son returned home from the hospital, I traveled to the northwest where he lived to assist in his recovery. I loved the two weeks I spent with him. Life had become a blur, but now I devoted all of my energy to my son. My worries were minimal in comparison to the challenges inherent in his medical recovery. Here in the Nebraska snow and cold, I felt far away from the sun and heat of my Arizona home. This change of scene allowed me to start to heal.

# An Angel Shows Up

○  ○  ○

As I worked closely with Paul, he methodically found clues to thread the chain of events together. He brought other federal officials to the case to secure more and more information. It turned out to be a very long, involved investigation, and I held out hope for some portion of restitution. More names started to surface, and the investigation grew more complex once it was determined the location of the scammer was outside the United States. Why did Carl request a change in location of the wired money? Paul was surely the sleuth we needed.

Since I had wired money, the federal postal inspector became involved in the case. My legwork began with filing reports and uncovering the details of my financial loss. I became nauseated again at the thoughts of traveling to mid-city amidst heavy traffic, unsure of the location of the government building. Paul kindly volunteered to take me there and introduce me to the inspector. As we traveled into mid-city and entered the government building, I was nervous and embarrassed, but thankful Paul was by my side.

We were invited into the conference room where we met Craig Torbenson, the federal postal inspector. His secretary greeted us with water bottles, which I was glad to have because my mouth felt like it was stuffed with cotton balls. Although I had felt nervous when I presented public seminars or taught in the classroom, I had never been paralyzed with this kind of fear.

Two more female staff members joined the meeting and I became even more nervous. Craig spoke first. He looked directly at me with little expression on his face and said, "Tell me your story." My thoughts raced like bees buzzing from one flower to another. I wanted to blurt out the entire story as quickly as possible. Anger had built up inside of me, and I was determined to find revenge. All these emotions felt like they were going to explode like a geyser going off in Yellowstone. I had a hard time organizing my thoughts until I remembered I had notes. Oh, yes. Read from your notes, Carole. I finally took some deep breaths and proceeded. Now I was on a mission. No tears. No anxiety. Simply facts, facts, and more facts. I had it all in my notes, and they were impressed!

Looking back on that day, I was blessed to have Craig come on the case. He was caring but got to the point. My background in health care taught me how to be caring, but I knew very little about fraud—a term I'm now very familiar with. Craig's role as the federal postal inspector became a very important part of this case although it was not apparent to me at the time. Over the span of two to three years, we corresponded with details of his findings, and I would have his ever-faithful assistance in filing charges. He stayed steadfast on the case and turned up an abundance of evidence that was hard to believe

Craig gave me a list of things to do. First, I needed to file fraud charges at the bank. All my money was wired from my bank to a Malaysian bank and the Bank of America in Sacramento. I was well aware that dealing with the Malaysian bank would be a dead end. I kept thinking, if I could somehow gain restitution from the last two amounts wired to Sacramento, I would be thrilled and feel a little less shame.

I left that meeting, feeling calmer and confident that the next step would be a little easier. The entire Federal Postal Service staff was helpful and compassionate, but at the same time, it was necessary for me to do my part for the plan to proceed. They asked many questions, filed notes, and wrote reminders of what must take place. Because I had wired money, this would be a federal case. That worked in my favor. Federal charges could be filed.

The next day, I gathered information detailing dates, dollar amounts, names of banks, addresses, and what I believed were the reasons for all of these payments. It was all neatly secured in my business binder. I was about to get the SOB. I felt confident and ready to proceed.

It was a brisk, sunny morning in January of 2013. I entered the Bank of America, with my head held high and a self-assured stride. I was a woman on a mission. An employee in the lobby welcomed me, and I calmly and professionally said, "I would like to speak to the manager, please." She said, "I am sorry, ma'am. She isn't available at the moment, but you could visit with the assistant manager." As I waited in line at the teller counter, I reviewed my prepared questions and answers. I knew them as I had been asked them so many times. I felt composed, ready to go to battle on this criminal. I had a few other not-so-nice words to describe him rolling around in my mind.

When the assistant manager came forward, I explained my intention to file charges of fraud regarding money wired to another Bank of America location. However, she informed me the charges could not be filed there. I would need to file the charges at the bank where the money was sent. My heart sank at the thought of going through all of this again. I misunderstood the legal procedures. I felt like a hockey player sent to the penalty box. Well, I have never played hockey, but I had been sent to the corner to sit out many a time by my father. I had been a solid customer for over sixty years at Wells Fargo. I wired the money from them five times. My heart pounded with humiliation, fear, and embarrassment at the thought of going through this procedure with my bank.

I gathered up all my papers, preparing to leave the bank, when a lovely lady stepped up to the counter. She was well dressed and obviously held a high position at this bank. With a pleasant smile, she slipped a small note under my business binder. Very softly she said, "This is a note that may be helpful for you and for us as well. It was dropped from an unknown angel." With those words, she turned and left.

Before I left, I asked the assistant manager, "Was that lady your manager?" She kindly replied, "Yes, she is our manager, and she is an outstanding woman."

As I read the note in my car, it all made sense. The note revealed the location of the Sacramento Bank of America. It also stated the individual named on the account with her personal address, vital information for our case. Up until this time, I had only the account name and bank location. Upon further investigation, we discovered the account had two addresses for this person. One was the bank address, the other was her personal home address. The "angel" brought forth more information than could possibly be imagined at the time.

Angels are present with many messages if we just listen and watch for them. I truly believe this message of hope and information was all part of this lesson in my life. A very small piece of paper given to me with hand-written information, at the most crucial time, opened the case of one of the largest online frauds located in both Nigeria and United States.

# Investigation, Warrant Served, Charges Filed

○ ○ ○

The federal postal inspector began his investigation by contacting officials in Sacramento. The California Department of Justice, Special Crimes Unit, was specifically contacted to investigate Marchetta Dycus, the individual named in the note. Within a few days I received a phone call from the special agent, Debra, who was assigned to the case.

Debra asked me to gather all the documented evidence of the wired money and emails stating Carl's request for money. She was a dynamic woman, full of passion and determination. She said, "I want to make it clear; I will do everything in my power to help you. This will be my mission to file charges, take the case to court, and see this person receives punishment for being a part of this widespread crime." She was relentless in pursuing all the evidence. Not only was she investigating every corner to find answers, she kept me posted about what was happening by phone and email. Even if nothing was moving forward, she kept me informed to let me know she was hard at work.

As I prepared the many receipts of wired dollars and withdrawals from my accounts, humiliation threatened to overwhelm me. Many times, I would have to stop for a few hours to recover from shockwaves of weakness that enveloped me before I had the energy to proceed again. The emails made me sick. I visually scanned many of them to gather important facts, but it felt painful and disgusting. I avoided reading details as much as possible. Recalling each request and rereading the words, dripping with romantic pleas for my help, made me wonder how I could have been so blind.

Stacking them quickly, I literally stuffed them into a registered package to be sent to the Sacramento Department of Justice as quickly as possible to get them out of my sight. I was humiliated, but at the same time grateful for the professionals who approached this work with dedication and sincere compassion. I wondered how many others they had seen suffer through this devastation. I later learned through our conversations together that there are many others with similar stories. Debra investigated other scams, but not to the extent that she was involved with mine. Although many share their horror stories with the public, even more people lock these traumas deep within their hearts. Charges are never filed. The embarrassment is too overwhelming for them to admit ever being a victim.

It seemed an eternity before Debra notified me that Ms. Dycus had been served a search warrant. Yes, a search warrant. There was actually a physical person to investigate. I had been waiting eagerly to see what they would find. Would they discover any of the money? What did she buy with my money? Was it sent directly to Carl in Malaysia? Who was this woman who was about to be arrested? What was ABL Distributions?

The search revealed alarming evidence. After I talked with Debra, I started to feel as if I might recover some of my financial loss. They found receipts of money received with my name on them. They also uncovered purchase receipts for six automobiles. Six automobiles? What would she do with all of those cars? In Ms. Dycus' file, they found a list of six people (which later increased to eight victims besides me) in this ring of criminal activity. Ms. Dycus also purchased large quantities of electronic equipment with the money I wired as well as money from the other victims. Special agents and investigators found more evidence of other suspected criminals involved with Ms. Dycus and Carl from this ongoing search warrant.

Ms. Dycus was signing signatures as Marchetta Dycus, Marchetta Caesar, and Marqita Dycus. Her ABL Distribution website was a front for a false company called Abundant Life Ministries. Soon the mystery of ABL

Distribution became clear. The address and ABL initials, which I had many times asked Carl, "What does ABL mean? Why am I sending money now to Sacramento?" I now knew. Abundant Life Distribution was abbreviated as ABL. It appeared as Abundant Life Ministries for their solicitations of church contributions.

In our investigation, we eventually found that the ABL bank account was linked to a website, where these criminals pretended to be a religious organization. Online donations were deposited regularly. Another member of the ring posed as a minister for this fraudulent organization. It was a depot for laundering money with the online dating ring. A piece of information, like a sparkling jewel uncovered unexpectedly from a deep hole, had been handed to me from the "Angel" bank manager. Marchetta Dycus was a name now in our vocabulary and a suspect for this crime. Our investigation was about to take on a new quest. We now had a suspect in the United States to help put pieces of the puzzle together. My heart pounded with excitement at the thought of restitution for my financial loss. Regaining even a small amount of this money would be most welcome.

However, I didn't realize there would be much more to unravel in this web of destruction. During this time, Carl had also conned seven other women and one man. He was a master at professional scamming, and he had a network of people helping him. We knew of at least two people working for him, and there were most likely many more.

Ms. Dycus' main contact in Malaysia and other countries was a man named Solomon. His passport indicated that he had made many trips from Malaysia to London, Nigeria, and Newbie, to name a few. With multiple contacts in various locations, this "ring" of people allowed Solomon to ship and receive all over the world. It was shockingly clear that Solomon and Carl were working together with others around the world scamming eight or more women and men at the same time they were scamming me. Sitting shoulder to shoulder in coffee houses in Nigeria and various countries, these con men used their laptop computers to create a magical bounty of staggering amounts. They focused on victims who were fifty and over from all walks of life.

Solomon had a significant role. His title in ABL Distribution was "Clergyman Solomon." Would faithful television viewers and website participants, of Abundant Life Ministries, question someone with the title of Clergyman Solomon? Of course not. Donations came from viewers who became faithful to the preaching of God and donated generously. The website was beautifully designed and, of course, user friendly. With taped messages holding viewers captive with their religious messages for weeks, donations came in generously. Who would question a contribution being sent to Bank of America, attention ABL Distribution and Clergyman Solomon? It was a distribution for sure—a distribution of cash to their pockets. Merchandise was purchased to enhance their lifestyle in the United States as well as being shipped to other countries. These television and computer viewers were caught in a net, just as the lonely hearts of women and men were caught and reeled in. It was obvious the TV viewers were being scammed of their donations to fund money for purchase of merchandise to support the ring. This was another link in the chain of these con artists.

My goal was to secure the car titles, sell the cars, and reduce some debt. Little did I know at the time that "the cars" would become a never-ending topic of conversation among my family, law officials, and friends as I continued along this quest.

# Starting to Heal in My Sanctuary

○ ○ ○

With patience, honesty, and doing the very best he could for me, my realtor, Ben, sold my home mid-summer. Ben had been my realtor when I had purchased the house. He had cared for my home when I traveled. He knew my home well, and, as a dear friend, I could tell him my story in confidence. Even though it wasn't the best time to sell a home in Phoenix, and he was under a deadline during the heat of the summer, Ben did the best he could for me in the sale.

It was now six months after learning of the scam. I was trying to work to the best of my ability every day. Looking for a new location was depressing and overwhelming. Had I made the right decisions regarding bankruptcy? My family continued to stand by me with encouraging words of support and advice. By late summer I found a rental property. Moving in September 2013, I started a new beginning.

Focusing on my work with Randall Designs was a major part of my life. Striving for financial security and sustaining mental stability consumed me. After I sold my house, leaving my friends and my familiar neighborhood, I suffered through a brutal rollercoaster of depression. Having to work fulltime motivated me to get out into the world. It would have been easier to become a shut-in and wither in my depression.

Fortunately, my new home became my sanctuary. With a private pool and many birds, it gave me the solitude to meditate. With my passion for floral design, I settled into planting flowers and adding hummingbird feeders to bring God's creatures close to me.

Drinking coffee at my dining room table, gazing at the pool, I felt the serenity of the water with its movement in the breeze, as though it was trying to brush away my sorrow. The quail, roadrunners, hummingbirds, doves, and wrens were constant visitors. They created a melody that changed every day. How can one be sad when you see God's work revealed in the magical hummingbird? Seeing him hover at the feeder, hearing his drumming wings as he sucks quickly the drop of succulent juice that carries him through the air, reminded me of the many miracles surrounding us every moment.

I watched a pair of doves meet each morning and evening on top of the fence. Their dove call became so familiar, announcing their arrival at their usual meeting place. I found it comforting to observe their loyalty to one another, sitting almost motionless side by side for thirty minutes or more. Then, seemingly without any communication, they would both take wing at the same moment. It must be bird intuition.

The roadrunner would often come to my sliding door and look at me having coffee as if to say, "It's ok. Time will heal." Quail paraded around the pool with their new hatch of twelve to fifteen babies. These young quail would scurry about and then all at once fall in line as if they had heard a whistle to get their attention.

Flowers were my escape after work. I trimmed, watered, and frequently made new arrangements. I have had hibiscus plants for many years and marveled at their large bloom, so perfect like the bell of a trumpet.

Hibiscus blossoms are a lesson in life. Watching the tightly bound buds mature and finally open is like anticipating a rose slowly unfold in all its surprising beauty. Unlike the rose blossom, which stands in its regal beauty for days, the hibiscus blossom lasts just one day. It tells us, "The sun is upon me for a new day. As I open to the world to absorb all that is possible, I have only today, the NOW. Yesterday, my shriveled bloom fell to the ground. Tomorrow I will be closed and dying on the bush, but TODAY I am open to all that is around me and sharing the beauty God has provided." I was reminded once again in my life that NOW is all we can live for. Once I held that close and lived by it, the healing began.

# Part 3

## Conviction, Restitution, and Recovery

# Finding My Money and
# Automobiles on a Dock

O   O   O

As the investigation continued, we determined that all six autos—a 2002 Toyota, 2003 Land Rover, a 2003 Mercedes E-320, a 2008 Mercedes C-300, a 2010 Honda MP, and a 2010 Honda MP— were purchased with the money I wired to Carl, through Ms. Dycus. She just happened to be an employee of the Department of Motor Vehicles near her residence in Sacramento, California. Through her job, she was in a position to select well-priced vehicles to meet the requests coming from Nigeria, Malaysia, and other countries. Through the investigation, we also learned that these cars were loaded on a freighter, sitting at a dock in Savannah, Georgia, waiting to be shipped off to another country. They were detained, waiting for proper export papers, and would be released within a few days. Time was limited. Authorities would have to move quickly to recover them before shipment.

Craig left immediately for Savannah. He wasted no time in reaching the dock. With the legal papers in hand, he arrived just in time to halt the shipment of the cars. (Perhaps the Angel of Hope was with us again.) They were sitting on a transport cargo ship ready to be sent to Malaysia. Craig proceeded with his assignment of recovery, assessed the cars to be in fairly good condition, and had all the vehicles removed from the ship and transported to a postal facility parking lot. My big concern was a financial obligation of storage. If I were to claim them, would I be responsible for rental space? Thankfully, the federal postal service stored these cars without charge.

Craig called me when he returned to Arizona after his wild trip to Savannah's shipping site. In our conversation he said, "The titles for the autos were definitely found in Ms. Dycus's home at the time the warrant was served. Carole, I believe you could possibly receive some amount of restitution from selling the autos." I was excited. There was a bit of hope that I would recover some money from this horrible situation. I was now most definitely ready to stand up and fight these con artists. Since the evidence revealed my money had purchased them, it would seem most likely this would be in my favor.

The case was filed in 2013. Because these transactions occurred in two states and out of the country, all legal procedures moved in snail procession. It was questionable who the car titles were going to belong to, what charges were going to be filed and how many victims were initially involved. Who DID the cars belong to? How would they be sold for restitution? Logistics, legal titles, value of vehicles and how long they could stay at the present sight were all legitimate concerns. At one point I was given copies of the titles.

With excitement, I called an acquaintance, who is an auto dealer. I said, "Glen, would you look at some car titles and tell me something about them?" "Car titles," he shouted laughingly, "How many are you looking to buy?" Rather reluctantly, I said, "Well, it's a long story I will tell you some day. But for now, will you look at these six titles and see if you can tell what they are worth?" Agreeing wholeheartedly, still chuckling, he said, "Scan them over and I will take a look." With his estimate, it appeared they could bring $20,000 in an auction, if offered at the most lucrative auction site. Glen's friend, Joe, also has a great interest in cars. Both were involved in car racing, and they were very enthusiastic about this car adventure. Joe and Glen were now brainstorming together about how to swing the best deal. Embarrassed and feeling somewhat stupid about the whole story, I now shared this outrageous scenario with them. Other than my family, only a couple of my friends were aware of what I was going through. After a few conversations, it became a fascinating adventure to see how many dollars we could get from auctioning these cars.

We discussed all the angles of the best location for auction price, shipment, and overall financial gain—if any. Glen tossed out all kinds of ideas on auction locations. He said, "I will price the transport cost upon doing a comparison on auction sites. We do, however, have to know if they are legally yours." Receipts had been documented that part of my scammed money had purchased the cars. I felt I had possession. Final authority would have to be given. I obtained advice from the Federal Postal Department on how I could secure information about sales and shipment. Of course, there were still barriers to overcome. Actually, since the Federal Postal Department was securing their placement, it was to their advantage, if legal, for me to sell them.

By now the conversations were getting mingled with humor. We started giving each car a name and wondering where they had been in their "car lives." I always felt, if these cars could talk, they would have so many wild and fascinating tales to share. They had ended up in Georgia, sitting on a dock, and worried they were going to travel the ocean. They would land in some foreign land and have new owners. Who would be driving them? Making up imaginary stories about them helped ease my financial and emotional pain. I shared the humor with my family, and it gave us all a bit to laugh and joke about.

A year had passed now, and "the cars" were not in my possession. They had been moved initially from the dock, to a postal parking lot, and then to another postal parking lot, still in Savannah, Georgia. In my work, I traveled around the country. One trip was close to Savannah, so I decided to make a short side trip to visit "the cars." I contacted Joe, inquiring if he would like to see them. "WOW," he said. Did you get possession? Where are they?" Smiling to myself, I said, "No, they are still hanging out in Savannah waiting for me. I want to go visit and see what they're up to." I then made arrangements with the postal inspector in that area. It was surprisingly workable. He was very accommodating, taking time on a weekend to meet.

We met Dave, the postal inspector, at the postal parking lot. I could hardly believe I was now standing there, gazing at these dirty, sad-looking vehicles. What a journey so far. From California, to a freighter on the dock in Savannah, then removed from the freighter, transported to a postal lot, then loaded and transported to another postal lot where they presently were. Dave told me this post office building has been sold, and they will have to move the cars again. Where would they go this time?

These autos had been sitting for a year now and deteriorating very quickly in the sun, wind, and rain. As Joe stood, hands in his pockets, just gazing at these grimy pieces of metal, plastic, and rubber, he smiled and said, "So this is what you bought?" As we inspected them, one by one, it was apparent the value was minimal. Each had its own character about it, with no doubt a story of its own.

The Range Rover towered over the others. As we peered through the dusty windows (all vehicles were locked), we could see several custom de-signed compartments to hold small items. It was interesting that this vehicle appeared to have been used for off-road activity. I believe there could have been many stories about this huge character before it was ever purchased. The Toyotas and Honda each seemed to have a little smile. I think they were telling us, "We have many miles left in us because we are small and mighty." Once proud, I am sure, the faded blue Mercedes looked old and tired. As we pondered over each of them, we couldn't help but joke about where the next destination would be for these special vehicles. My thoughts went to dollar signs. Would I have to pay for the transport? None of these vehicles would start. They would have to be loaded on a transport. There had not been a new location established. But it was a federal case, and the inspector assured me the responsibility would rest on the postal department. I was very grateful to the officials who handled all of the transport procedures of these vehicles. They were most cordial in every way. I do believe they had heard the story and were as interested as myself to know the outcome.

I could see the curiosity in their facial expressions, as if to say, "What the Hell is going on with these cars and where will it end?" The final destination would either be an auction business or a salvage yard. I so hoped they would make it to the auction. But for now, they were autos on the move again, destination unknown.

o   o   o

In 2015, Debra, the special agent in Sacramento, retired. She had been consistently keeping me up to date on the pending charges towards Ms. Dycus. Her weekly phone calls and emails were detailed and supportive. Through communication from Debra, it was apparent there would be little or no movement from the law to pursue charges against Solomon or Carl. It was quite clear Solomon had been diligent with staying out of a paper trail to escape involvement with Ms. Dycus. Clearly, he was guilty of using the donated funds coming through ABL contributions. However, documentation of his purchases was lacking. He was interviewed by authorities on several occasions but had substantiating evidence to clear himself. Carl, with his stolen identity, was never located.

There were more times than not when just her message of "no progress" kept me hopeful. Not only was she communicative, but she was really dedicated to convicting Ms. Dycus. I kept her words in my mind, "Carole, we will work on this case until we find the evidence to convict and have some restitution for you."

The conviction process was long and drawn out. Since Debra's retirement and dedication to the case, communication had become minimal from the various legal departments. The district attorney in Sacramento was out of touch. There had been no contact since 2014. Arizona officials were no longer involved. I felt myself simmering on the back burner, which lowered my self-esteem even more. This case seemed to be cold and not of interest to anyone but me.

Officials in Arizona had asked me many times what sort of procedures were developing. None of us were getting information from the investigation that should have been taking place in Sacramento. Phone calls were not returned from the criminal investigator or the district attorney.

During the hot Arizona summer, in July 2015, I received a phone call from a gentleman named Scott. He introduced himself as "the third party appointed receiver." With rapid speech and little clarity, he explained his responsibility was management of the money received from sale of the autos and cash recovered in Ms. Dycus's home. He asked rather abruptly, "How much money did you spend for the autos and what was your total loss?" With great astonishment and shock, I was speechless. My heart was pounding. My thoughts began racing, "Will there be some dollars finally coming to me? Is this guy real or another fraud? Why after more than two years am I finally having this conversation? Why have I not received mail correspondence asking these questions? I was suspicious. The phone call seemed inappropriate.

After taking several breaths to calm myself, I finally started asking questions. He revealed to me there were ten individuals who were scammed at the same time by the same ring of con artists. Debra, the special agent, had previously told me there were receipts at the time of the search warrant showing my wired money had purchased the autos. But other electronic equipment had also been purchased with my wired money. Copies of the car titles had been sent to me by the Federal Postal Agency at an earlier date. My cash outlay was far more than the dollars that would possibly come from auto liquidation. I had proof of all wired money. Now I was being informed I would have to split all the money ten ways.

He said he had collected his data from the court documents. He offered no financial figures to verify the spending of my wired money, and it seemed to be a very unprofessional approach. A phone call? He didn't want written documentation of my wired money? He was asking verbal clarification. I was not sure of his identity.

Upon making several phone calls to the attorney general's office, leaving messages without returned calls, I finally, through various channels, was able to verify what had taken place; (a) a court order to restrain property and assets had been established against Ms. Dycus, and (b) assets had been established against Ms. Dycus to prepare for restitution.

It seemed like it was being handled as just another scam, no big deal. In spite of being the victim, I had been kept totally in the dark during court proceedings and treated like a bystander in a closed closet. I am sure the other nine were feeling the same. The court had used whatever documentation of dollars that they wanted. It appeared they would take the available dollars from auctioned cars and cash found in the house and subsequently divide it among the ten of us. Never at any time did I receive a request for documentation of my loss. Records were sent to the district attorney of Sacramento, but they appeared to have never reached the court or were ignored.

Scott, the appointed third party, notified me when the case was going to court. He was the only contact I had. I anxiously placed several phone calls to him hoping to learn what was happening with the hearing. The phone always went to voice mail. I left messages time after time, but I never got a response. I decided I needed to be more patient. He didn't provide me his email or any other source for contacting him. I was trusting no one at this point, and no one was informing me of the procedures being taken against Ms. Dycus.

The 2015 holidays came and went. 2016 arrived. The holidays moved on into spring. The long summer finally ended; the Arizona fall felt refreshing. Correspondence from the investigation was dormant once again. I worked long hours.

My job in sales and design took me flying out of the city to various parts of the country. Working with beautiful fabrics, assisting dancers with fittings, meeting challenges to please the professionals in all types of gowns. and always being with the public kept my mind occupied.

It was good therapy to travel, to be in a five-star ballroom selling beautiful gowns, but always wishing I was dancing. However, my focus was sales and financial recovery. At the end of the day, it was a struggle to keep the ugly memories away when you are in a hotel. Walls are not warm friendly arms hugging you.

There was still no news of encouragement. The thought of any restitution was not in my financial planning. It appeared hopeless for any financial return. I felt I would keep working and try to hold it together. I no longer danced competitively because of cost and working. However, I tried to dance socially to keep music in my life and movement in my soul.

During this time, I continued to deepen spiritually by living courageously, meditating, seeking daily guidance through inspirational books, hypnotism, and journaling of my ups and downs, to help me keep move on with daily life.

# News of Sentencing

Early November 2016, before the Thanksgiving holiday, I decided to make another call to Scott to inquire if there had been a settlement. Certainly, there should be some word since the last time I talked to him when he told me the court hearing was scheduled July 2015. I called with mixed feelings. I was hoping for good news, but I also felt guarded to avoid further disappointment.

He answered the phone, which surprised me, since he had avoided my calls previously. He was very vague and said, "You need to contact the district attorney of Sacramento, California. You can get his number from the website. I am no longer on the case." That was the end of the conversation.

I called the district attorney immediately and left a message on his voice mail. I requested information regarding the July 2015 court results for Ms. Dycus. I was hopeful for some news but leaving a voice mail wasn't very encouraging.

Three weeks later, on December 16th, I received a reply from my voice mail. It was not the District Attorney who returned the call. One of his office staff said, "I advise you to call the Department of Corrections, 877-----." Call ended. Three weeks to hear that? I made the call and was informed there was $87.00 that I could possibly receive in February 2017! EIGHTY-SEVEN DOLLARS? WHY BOTHER WITH THE POSTAGE TO MAIL IT? WHAT THE HELL? I'M SCAMMED AGAIN?

What was going on? I asked for information regarding the case. Her response was, "I'm sorry, Ms., but I cannot give out that information." I knew there had been a court hearing. I thought to myself, "What else has taken place that I don't know about?"

I asked about garnishing Ms. Dycus' wages because I thought maybe she was still working and no charges were filed! I was told that would not be possible, nor could I receive any of her Social Security. They also felt she was not working. I was then advised, "Call the Receiver of the case, Scott 916--------." WOW. Someone to finally talk to.

What was going on? I was not informed of her conviction, sentencing, restitution. . . nothing. Now I was to call Scott, who had told me he was no longer on the case? My head was spinning as I called Scott and asked him about any restitution.

"A check was mailed to you October 2016. You've never cashed it."

"I never received a check," I said. "Nobody told me about the charges or case number." After repeating my address to me, I let Scott know that address for me was correct. "I was never told the amount of restitution from the court results, or when Ms. Dycus went to court, or even when she was convicted. If you mailed a check for thousands of dollars, but it never got cashed, why didn't anyone catch that? And why didn't *you* or anybody else in law enforcement ever tell me about her conviction?" My voice kept getting louder until I was yelling at him.

His defense for why I was never told these things was to explain the final restitution for us all. "The cash value of the vehicles at auction was $6,000." Scott then told me that he had handled the journey of the autos at public car auction. My mind went immediately to these abandoned cars. Like orphans, they had been shipped, loaded, unloaded, and stored in holding lots behind locked gates since 2013. Held together by a common bondage, these cars had been victims of people peeking under their hoods. They had weathered hurricanes and investigators asking their worth. They had dealt with dirt and grime, aging paint, and had probably wondered if they would ever find an owner that valued them. Craig had so often taken charge of these cars' security and kept me informed about their location. Now, coldly, Scott said, "They were worth just $6,000." He had no idea how I felt about these "orphans." They had been my anchor of hope for some financial return. Somehow, I felt I had abandoned them. I wondered if they went to the junkyard.

Despite the plea bargain, it appears Ms. Dycus was not held accountable for any of the cash wired to her by victims like me. She was only held accountable for the automobiles that were confiscated and auctioned. Court documents from California show that police officers seized $7,495.00 from inside her house. Then they auctioned off $23,965 worth of goods to help pay restitution. The total available for restitution was $700,000, but they could never get that amount from her, so the total actually available for restitution, after administrative costs, amounted to $27,693 to be divided among ten victims based on the percentage each person lost. Because I lost the most, I got $10,709 of the $27,693. But we EACH lost a lot more than a few thousand dollars. The hundreds of thousands of dollars that I documented having lost to her, never reached the court. I doubt that any other victims received fair restitution either. Not only were we victims of con artists, we felt let down by the court system as well. To them, it was a guessing game about how much we, the ten victims, had sent to Carl and Ms. Dycus, even though we documented our losses. I still wanted to know where my $10,709 check was.

Our conversation ended on December 16, 2016, with Scott giving his word that he would be sending me a check the next day, December 17, 2016. He would also said he would send an email that day detailing the outcome of the charges and penalty. Ms. Dycus's conviction and sentencing had taken place a whole year before on August 25, 2015. Obviously, none of us victims were a high priority of the justice system. Scott didn't even send the check registered or priority mail. It arrived December 23, 2016 in a plain envelope, with my address and a return address poorly hand written, but I finally had the check for $10,709 in my hands.

Where had all my money been lurking for a year and a half? The restitution was nothing compared to my total loss of $400,000.00 to both Carl and Ms. Dycus. However, I now believe the words of Mike Dooley from the Universe, "No matter how much money or love you've made or lost, you can still make more."

On July 15, 2015, Marchetta Ann Dycus had pleaded no contest to the following charges: White Collar Crime Enhancement: (a) Embezzlement, (b) Fraud, (c) Identity Theft, (d) Grand Theft, (e) Criminal Profiteering, and (f) Conspiracy. A Harvey Waiver, which allows a court to consider dismissed charges, was entered.[3] Restitution orders were agreed on for the victims. She was sentenced to three years and four months in state prison.

Ms. Dycus served a partial sentence, approximately one year, and was ultimately released on probation. The reason for early release: "California prisons are overcrowded."

# Shame, Anger, Humiliation

Once the whole ordeal was finalized with that measly check, I experienced many sleepless nights, and the same dreams repeated themselves over and over. In my previous travels to Africa, I saw strong women carrying heavy loads. I kept seeing these beautiful African women night after night. I could see them in their colorful dresses, and feel them trudging barefoot through the rough, dusty, uneven terrain. Their strong bodies walking tall, balancing two large containers of water, one on each end of a pole over their shoulders. Often, they had a basket of grain on top of their head as well. They had to carefully balance their loads to preserve every drop of precious water they were taking to their families. They seemed to walk with pride, strength, and with purpose.

Over these difficult years I felt weighted down like them and I could feel it affected my posture. My entire body felt heavy. I was not the dancer with the tall posture that I had once been. I wanted to walk tall and strong like the African women again. Often my steps felt they were sinking into mud. My shoulders drooped, rounding and turning inward, away from the world. My balance was physically unsteady at times, and I felt out of balance in life. My soul's passion for dancing had ceased. Stifled and buried deep in my depressed body, it was only a long-ago memory. It was a struggle to get out of bed in the morning. For many years, I walked tall as a nurse. I was proud and happy to be a mother and as a child, I was proud to put in a good day's work. The creative talents I surfaced after my divorce went underground and yet cried out, "Hey, don't we have a place in this life anymore?" Theses agonizing years were burdened with shame, guilt, and low self-esteem.

I have worked these retirement years, but not by choice. My friends ask, "Why are you still working?" I usually replied, "I like keeping my mind and body active." However, the thoughts racing in my mind said, " Yes, I like working and staying active, but it takes on a different feeling when you need the finances."

Eventually I decided to leave the ballroom wear business. The overwhelming amount of travel ended up exhausting me. I returned to an arm of the healthcare field. After passing the state exam for health insurance, I am currently licensed as an independent benefits advisor. I am grateful to God each and every day for giving me the strength and good health to continue to work. Without the loving support of my family, I would not have climbed the many mountains I faced during these challenges.

How often the quote comes to my mind from Mike Dooley, "Do you know what's a million times better than getting to the TOP OF THE MOUNTAIN? GETTING THERE AFTER HAVING BEEN LOST."[4] Certainly, I was lost. Now that I'm at the top of the mountain it feels tremendous.

As I share this profound experience, I feel the mask of false security finally crumble away. It has felt like a mud facial, thick and heavy for many years. Much care is given in removing mud facials so not to disturb the refreshed new appearance that has developed under that mask. The age lines and wrinkles are less pronounced after a facial. With the mask of false security removed, my expression of sadness has been replaced with a smile of dignity and self-worth. Joy exudes from my soul once again. Strength from spiritual study, working with several spiritual healers, meditation, study and use of hypnotism during those troubled years empowered me to regain my self-worth and rise above the shame and guilt. Happiness and joy fill my heart now.

WHY DID I CHOOSE SUCH A CHALLENGING LESSON? The

reason became clear as I matured spiritually finding different ways to heal. One of the most difficult challenges I faced was forgiving the evil person who perpetrated this scam on me, severely wounding my heart and lowering my self-esteem. I learned to forgive is to heal and move forward. You must forgive before you can heal. I walk with pride and carry this "assignment" with love.

A quote from The Indian Spiritual Leader, Sri Chinmoy states, "Life is nothing but the expansion of love."[5] But, we must have our own vessel filled and keep refilling it before we can share so generously with others. Through what has seemed an uphill struggle with an empty vessel many times, I have evolved into an authentic, empowered woman. Gary Zukav details characteristics of the authentically empowered personality as humility, clarity, forgiveness, and love. He states, "a micro-checklist for creating authentic power would include TRUST, RELAX, DO YOUR BEST, AND ENJOY YOURSELF."[6] Certainly nothing on this micro-checklist was easy. Our lives have a purpose, and often it takes nearly a lifetime to recognize lessons put before us. The autumn years, or perhaps they are winter years for me now, brought me this awakening. Being one of the statistics of on-line dating scam was not on my bucket list for retirement. It was difficult to become one of the consumers who lost more than $230 million in 2016."[7]

Sri Chinmoy stated, "The moment you know who you really are, all secrets of the world will be an open book to you."[8] I feel the freedom of knowing who I am. Learning to live in the Now has brought peace. Being transparent, fully examining and taking responsibility for a tragedy such as this awakens one's self. Has it been painful? Yes, and hard work.

I have read and studied Eckhart Tolle. I believe I have found my "Presence" and become free of identification of my "pain-body." As described by Tolle, "People with strong pain-bodies often reach a point where they feel their life is becoming unbearable, where they can't take any more pain, any more drama."[9] I had so many memories of pain. The loss of money was only one of the many. For seven years, the secret and shame of being scammed stayed buried in my heart. Revealing this experience to others showing how it is possible to rise above it, I have taken charge of not identifying with it nor allowing it to be my identification. Whether it be from an online dating scam, an identity theft, an abusive relationship, or overwhelming guilt, all these experiences can leave thousands of people feeling downright stupid. The light of Presence now lives within me. It is clear, blessings will be tenfold, as I strive to teach, share, lead with compassion, and stay true to myself.

In my journey, it took many months before my spiritual growth became powerful enough to rise above this tragedy. I worked hard, meditating, breathing, reading, and studying many lessons of various spiritual leaders. I now walk tall in my sanctuary and speak each day with my living creatures that surround me. I believe they know my story and have brought their songs of healing. As I sit on my patio, they often fly very close to me and hover for a while as if to say, "See, I told you it would be alright. You have learned to be patient and self-aware. You have learned to love yourself and elevate your self-esteem. You have become enlightened to that which is around you and within. Now you're ready to share your story with others."

My wish for you is to love yourself, protect yourself from a broken heart, and live life. My physical body is tall again, my soul beams God's light even brighter than before. I speak now and share, knowing there are many others with secrets deep in their hearts. You too can win the battle that may seem so ugly and never ending. The sun will shine again. The lotus, in all its serenity, will bloom as it rises slowly from murky waters. Roots are present deep in the water, just as love is present deep in your heart waiting for nourishment and to be shared. Allow your life to bloom! Take back your power! Tell your story! Live your life with love!

# Part 4

● ○ ● ○ ●

## How to Protect Yourself

Women get scammed online for three reasons: love, loneliness, and low self-esteem. In this section, I will explain how all three reasons, in combination, can make women especially vulnerable to being scammed. Then I'll share more about how you can grow personally and learn how to better protect yourself from fraud.

# Love

Dating online can be an addiction of love. Brian Hay has stated, "The strongest drug in the world is love. The scam bastards know that and can get away with it."[10] We are born with love in our soul. As life progresses, we long to share our love with others as well as love ourselves. Whether it is loving our child from birth to eternity or finding a love with a companion to share our life, we know it is delicate and yet very strong. We want to love and be loved. What is the meaning of love? Why is it so addictive?

Our souls hold within us a fountain of love. Indian Spiritual Teacher, Sri Chinmoy, says, "If love means to possess someone or something, then that is not real love, not pure love. If love means to give oneself, to become one with everything and everyone then that is real love."[11] We are ready to give and want the same in return. However, if we have not experienced being loved from childhood into adulthood, the full meaning of love is not felt nor understood.

The need to be loved, to love yourself, and to give love in return are extremely powerful emotions. The hurt that may be felt with the lack of feeling loved triggers pain for years ahead in life. That suffering we feel, if not expressed, may be buried for years, and becomes a constant trigger in our lives. However, to love thy self holds the power to love others and be loved. Hearing the phrase "I love you" can give us strength in life, but it is sometimes spoken to satisfy the other person's desire to hear the words.

Wanting to hear "I love you" from someone can become a long-held desire. Also, this feeling of love is often locked inside of the heart, unable to be spoken. Love is necessary in our lives. If we do not love ourselves, we cannot love others. The strong desire then to be loved and love someone be-comes a constant chase, a longing, often an obsession. Loving ourselves can be the most difficult challenge, and it must come first to open our hearts to allow loving others and to experience our self-esteem.

# Loneliness

Senior widows or divorced, middle aged women aren't the only ones who long for companionship and love. "People think victims are all lonely old women who can't get a date," says Barbara Sluppick, who founded the Romance Scam Organization in 2005. She says she has seen "doctors, lawyers, and police officers" get scammed too. She further states, "Online dating scamming is now over a $2 billion industry."[12]

The power of reading the message of love tugs at the heart with more emotion than speaking face to face. Remember the World War 11 era? Love letters were very powerful. Those in the military, separated from their sweethearts or wives thousands of miles away, sent handwritten letters over the oceans. Each lover filled the empty and lonely days and nights with only the tattered letters to read over and over. Loyalty to their loved ones kept them faithful when reading these romantic words. Many long-awaited letters were kept in special places, like specially-decorated shoe boxes or in a military pack, tucked away to read and keep close to their hearts. The romantic poetry and promising words were locked in portions of their hearts and the strong bond of love kept hope alive of someday being together. Love letters soothed the loneliness.

This computer age of romance brings a strong message through words and video unlike ever before. Instead of the letter arriving in the mail, computer keyboards come alive all hours of the day and night waiting for that special message to pop up. Pictures of the lover are readily available, often sexually attired. The online dating services for men are often dependent on availability of women to form a group. The organized group of predators, often working from the same room of computers, have a list of several available women to participate in the scams. A woman is notified when there is an interested man online. Step by step, she then becomes a part, of the scam. Pictures are sent, and the image can be enlarged to the point where it often feels like this new suitor is in the room with you. These sensual pictures, videos, and romantic poems of love enhance these long-distance relationships.

Instead of the picture carried on the battlefield, dirty and wrinkled, yet carefully tucked in a safe and secret place, these emails now can be seen and read multiple times and interpreted how you want to see and feel them. They are kept, never to be lost. Dreamy expectations fill each day the lover is away, and an eagerness to meet becomes an obsession.

Psychologist Monica Whitty explains, "Computer-mediated relationships can be hyper-personal—more strong and intimate than physical relationships."[13] Because the parties are not meeting in real life out in the world, they can control how they present themselves. They can create idealized avatars that command more trust and closeness than their true selves. The result being, that by seeing the written text and reading it over and over again, the bond grows stronger. No matter what our circumstance, even if we have a stable, well-paying job, supportive friends and family, and a comfortable home, we can become obsessed in a quest for love and companionship. When loneliness creeps in, joy is absent. Women and men of all ages then seek love to fill that emptiness. It doesn't matter if you are a retired widow sitting at home, a professional woman lawyer looking for a mate, or the divorced male CEO sitting in his office on Wall Street, wanting a companion once again. If it's absent from our lives, our souls are seek love.

# Low Self-Esteem

Self-esteem is an essential part of human life That determines how people interpret their own value, whether in terms of personality or physical appearances. People with low self-esteem are said to not value themselves very highly. This can often lead to depression or may pave the way to a destructive path in life. The opposite can be the case in people with high self-esteem. They may be high achievers, value themselves very highly, and less likely to become depressed. Self-esteem is not a permanently locked-in mental trait.

Falling on hard times of financial loss, a breakup of a marriage, losing a job, altered health, and change in body image can all cause lower self-esteem. Finding solutions to elevate self-esteem may be a rocky journey. Often building relationships is a major challenge on this upward climb. Seeking a relationship online allows the individual to communicate without the intimidation of face-to-face interaction in the world. People who come to this situation wounded in some way are vulnerable to online dating scams.

Online scamming professionals recognize low self-esteem personalities seeking love and will latch on very quickly. The scam artist looks out for in profiles where the person is a lonely heart and has money. Lonely hearted people want to find love and build a relationship with a companion to enjoy things like financial security and help restore their self-esteem. Online scamming pros know this and can hook their vulnerable victims quickly and easily.

# Modern Technology

○ ○ ○

Technology has changed online dating by becoming a powerful tool for scamming victims out of thousands and even millions of dollars. Since the 1990s, this criminal activity has become an over $2 billion industry. The Federal Trade Commission reported that online scams doubled between 2013 and 2014, with one in ten being scammed. "This figure is no doubt low, because many are not reported. Online relationships can elevate very powerful and more quickly, affecting the boundaries of 'real' and online relationships."[14] In my research about online fraud, I came across information about Enitan, another con man engaged in this activity in Niegeria.[15] Reading about how Enitan, who now lived in fear, helped me understand this criminal world better. In the article. Enitan speaks out against the practice of scamming. "Once you are out of the game," he explains, "you are seen as a traitor. You become the enemies of those who are in it.'[16]

Born in Benis, a neighboring area near Lagos, Enitan and his family moved to Nigeria during his childhood. As he looked for opportunities in the emerging powerhouse of Africa's most populous nation, he found "the game," Nigeria's shadow economy of fraudulent activity. These scams were typically referred to as "advance-fee" frauds, where unsuspecting strangers were promised of riches to be paid to in exchange for a modest payment. First, the stranger would receive letters, then texts, and emails, all apparently from Nigerian officials. Over time, this scam became well known. In our current society, these con artists have adopted a more effective strategy— mining dating sites to target their next victims.

Enitan says "ignorance and desperation" drove him to fraud in 2004, when he was eighteen years old. He estimated in over four years that he made "more than $800,000.00 from about 20 victims, both women and men." Then he drifted into working with other Nigerian men known as the "Yahoo Boys," a ring of criminals who conducted their business from free Yahoo.com email accounts. Enitan learned how to be a con man from older mentors and passed it on to younger friends. The excessive corruption in the country, political instability, and high rate of unemployment made this criminal game very tempting.

In describing their methods, Enitan explained that the scamming begins with a stolen identity. Using stolen credit card numbers, the scammer would flood the dating sites with fake profiles. They moved from the dating site to Yahoo.com email very quickly to avoid detection of the stolen credit card. Victims could be found anywhere. Scammers also looked for connections on social media, but dating services provided the most fertile territory. Profile photos were pirated from social media or other dating sites. Enitan says, "It is always better if the prospective woman makes the first move. Then we do not have as much challenge to convince them of our trust. We know then that there is something they like about us." To snare women, he'd pose as older men, financially secure, and often as someone who worked in the military or in engineering. For male victims, he just needed a photo of an alluring younger woman. "Guys are easier to convince," he says. "They're a bit desperate for beautiful girls. The common thread between them: **loneliness.**" All victims, Enitan says, were divorced or widowed. The lonely heart is a vulnerable heart.[17]

# Be Your Own
# Private Detective

○ ○ ○

I have shared my story with you. Now I want to give you tips on how to detect fraud and be your own private detective. I will point you in the direction of how and where to date safely and confidently online.

## Background Check Sources

The following websites are examples of available resources for researching online users. In all matters of background checking, keep in mind there is a limit to the ability and requirements of an online resource's accuracy and the currency of any criminal status of a person.

In addition to these resources, you must use your own personal judgment when deciding to meet a stranger. Educate yourself as much as possible about ways to protect yourself from scammers so that you can be as self-reliant as possible.

### Truthfinder
https://www.truthfinder.com

Truthfinder is a public records service with an A+ rating from the Better Business Bureau and over 14,000 5-Star reviews on Google Play. Some of the information available includes police records, criminal records, contact information, photos, and social media activity, as well as volumes of information available to search a person's background. Data comes from the government. Background checks tend to be highly accurate, although there is no 100 percent guarantee on all reports. The price of a background check varies with the package you choose. Buying a standard membership will provide you with unlimited reports through Turthfinder. You can buy a membership for just one or two months and call to cancel at any time.

## TinEye

https://www.tinEye.com

With TinEye, you can uncover scams using images that you upload to the site. It's also often used to search out catfish scams and to look for lost loved ones.

## Google Images

https://images.google.com

You can use Google Images to check the authenticity of a profile. After copying the person's profile picture from the online dating site, you can conduct a reverse-image search with the Google Images link. Through this research, you can check to see if the name, address, and physical description match the information provided on the online dating site. If there are discrepancies, this person most likely used a stolen identity to engage in further fraudulent activity.

## Romance Scams

https://aarp.org/money/scams-fraud

This AARP website offers information to those who fear there are being scammed. An experienced volunteer is available to take your call and assist you in contacting authorities. The service is free to AARP members as well as nonmembers and currently available on weekdays from 7:00 a.m. to 11:00 p.m. ET. Phone 877-908-3360.

## Scamalytics

https://scamalytics.com/

Scamalytics maintains the largest shared anti-fraud database dedicated to the online dating industry.[18] This is a source for a blacklist of scammers using false pictures. It reveals current and previous scammers. It is widely used as an antifraud solution to help online dating businesses moderate scammers automatically. For personal info you may Click on https://scamalytics.com/ip/ to see the latest scammer and fraud.

## Instant Checkmate

https://www.instantcheckmate.com

Instant Checkmate and Truthfinder offer similar data for membership. With 100 percent confidentiality, your search will provide (a) social media profiles (b) online presence and activity, (c) criminal record, (d) Driving Under the Influence incidences, (e) place of residency and confirms U.S. citizenship, (f) military service (g) living multiple personalities (h) court records. You can choose from three membership options. Upfront billing is required when you sign up on the internet. Instant Checkmate has been given an A+ by the Better Business Bureau.

## Top4 Background Checks

https://www.top4backgroundchecks.com

On this website, you can compare four public records service companies that perform background checks. The top four on this site include two I have already mentioned (Instant Checkmate and Truthfinder), along with two new ones (Seek Verify and Intelius). These sites are examples of where you can do research, but they provide only pieces of information to broaden your knowledge about individuals from available sources.

## Be Aware

**Language:** Does his vocabulary, grammar, and his accent correspond with the country he claims as home? Do his emails, reflect his verbal conversations with the same grammar and accent.?

**Flowery Language:** Does he immediately shower you with romance? Consider that to be a warning.

**Hesitancy:** Does he seem uncomfortable or hesitate when you ask him details about his life? Ask him specifics about where he lives. See if he can provide information that would back up what he has said about his background.

**Social Media:** If he is on social media, check his network of friends. Are they people who seem consistent with what you know about him? If possible, talk with a few of his friends. Reach out to them directly. Don't ask him to connect you with them.

**Email Address:** Romance scams make available scammer emails. Check his email address before leaving the dating site. Inquire about why he left the online service. Be very cautious when someone communicates with you off the site.

**Inconsistent:** Take notes for inconsistencies in his stories. Document pertinent information, compare, and check for inconsistencies of all areas in his profile.

**Take Your Time:** Do not let your experience of romance cloud your judgment. One of the best ways to protect yourself from your own emotional vulnerability is to take your time to conduct adequate research. A scammer will quickly start to romance his victim in the hopes of immediately building trust. A good relationship is worth waiting for. Heed the warning signs at all cost.

**Meeting:** If you decide to meet, choose a local public place that you know. Let a friend know the location, date, and time when you will be meeting your date.

## Research Online Dating Sites

Not all dating sites are scams, but not all are safe! Keep in mind that just in the United States itself, there are more than 2,500 dating websites. "Every year, over 1,000 are being added. There are over 8,000 dating websites all over the world."[19] When enrolling in an online dating service, you should check to see if there is contact information for the website in case you need any assistance or support. Scam websites often fail to provide any way for you to contact them. However, you also need to be aware that scam artists can be found on legitimate online dating services. These criminals will be wherever they can find lonely hearts.

Before choosing an online service, check if the dating site is a member of the Online Dating Association (ODA). According to ODA, "Membership means that the site has to commit to an industry code of practice that includes honest communication with users, protecting their privacy and providing a mechanism for reporting abuse. Inclusion of the ODA's logo on the site indicates membership." A reputable dating site can act to get people removed from the site immediately to help safeguard you and other prospective victims. "If you have been asked for money, verbally abused or experienced behavior in any inappropriate manner, report to the ODA immediately."[20] ODA Member websites monitor the site but they still need to be told if you see a profile that contains obscenity, pornography, or other offensive information. Once you notify a site, they will act to remove the content and the user. At the moment that you witness abusive behavior, you should stop corresponding with the person immediately and contact your local police, as well as ODA. Your local police will assist you in filing charges through the appropriate law enforcement.

I will mention only a few online dating sites, giving an example of how they can vary in interest for members. With thousands of existing sites to choose from, be wise and make careful choices based on the criteria I've mentioned so far and on your own personal interests. For example, one on-line dating service, "How About We" (www.howaboutwe.com) offers what they call "Offline Dating." Through this service, participants suggest "Date Ideas," a place to meet and activities to do. In this way, members can begin dating with less preliminary online interaction. If you're looking for a long-term relationship or marriage, other dating websites you might consider include eHarmony.com, Match.com, MatchSeniors.com, or Chemistry.com.[21]

There are also several dating site apps available through Google. One of these apps, Tinder, claims to be the "World's Hottest App" with 20 billion matches to date and 26 million matches a day. Many people have success-fully used apps like Tinder and online dating websites to find love. I hope the same for you. But please use the advice and resources I've provided to help you protect yourself from fraud.

# Red Flags That You're Being Scammed

○  ○  ○

By sharing my story with you, I have shown how a person can be scammed out of hundreds of thousands of dollars. In this section of my book, I want to provide you a quick summary of the red flags to watch out for as warnings that you are being scammed. Even when women know that something looks suspicious, they can still be vulnerable and be victimized by criminals in the process I describe below. I'm highlighting these red flags here because they are an important reminder of what to watch out for, especially when you're lonely and looking for love.

**Personal Emails:** Do not leave a dating service until you have met a man in person. He may strongly encourage you to switch to communicating through personal emails. Often, through this correspondence, the perpetrator intensifies the romance very quickly. Since you have stopped communicating on site, the online service is no longer monitoring your conversations.

**Smothering with Affection (Brainwashing):** You receive romantic emails, seductive phone calls, and beautiful flowers from him. Oftentimes, you hear from him many times a day.

**Financial Request/Emergency Situation:** The perpetrator tells you that he is in dire needs of funds. An emergency has occurred. He could be out of the country. As his potential victim, you may already be emotionally invested, so you are especially vulnerable to financial "emergencies" from someone you have "fallen in love with." He often accompanies his financial requests with romantic vows, dreams of a future together, and plans for future meetings with you.

**Failure to Show Up:** The perpetrator says he has to cancel your plans to meet. Oftentimes, the reason he cannot come is because he has a new financial predicament. He will likely ask for more money and make new plans with you to meet. During this time, he will also continue sending you daily emails, romantic videos, and phone calls full of sweet romance. He may even send flowers again.

**Transfer of Money:** The perpetrator promises to pay you back very soon with interest. Soon, you believe you will replace your loneliness with companionship. You feel like you are investing in a future together.

**Further Money Transfers:** The perpetrator's requests for money become more frequent. The dollar amount could be as much as $100,000.00 per request. If you have already sent thousands of dollars, he has successfully gained your trust. You likely believe you are totally in love. He knows this, so he continues to elaborate on his story to keep you enthralled.

**Fear and Doubt:** You have now spent all of your life's savings. Every time you were supposed to meet him, this criminal comes up with an excuse to not show up. You have likely told no one about this relationship and your investment in it. You feel ashamed and stupid, but you still love him, so you're afraid to lose him, and you're also afraid to find out the truth or to share about your experience with people who could help you.

**Tears, Pleas and Further Requests:** He continues to ask you for more money, telling you that he is in a desperate situation, that he can't wait to see you when this is all over, and that he will pay you back with interest. You tell him that you can't send him any more money. He becomes angry. Your lonely heart gives in once more, and you send more money.

**Money Chase:** You may think, "If I stop now, I will never get my money back. If I continue, the authorities will help me recover my money." Meanwhile, the perpetrator will continue to take all he can from you until you finally stop sending him funds.

**File a Claim and Get Support***:* Once you finally stop giving what you now realize is a criminal your money, you may still not be sharing your experience with friends and family. You could feel broken hearted and in grief. The loss of self-worth, shame, guilt, financial stress, depression, and extreme loneliness can feel overwhelming. While you may still feel like you must keep your experience a secret, you should file a complaint with FBI'S Internet Crime Complaint Center (https://www.ic3.gov/default.aspx). You should also get support immediately. Confide in the any family members and friends who will love you no matter what. Don't be afraid to reach out. You will need and you deserve their support.

## Another Warning

**Criminals' "Sucker" list:** If you have filed a claim, or even if you have not, as a victim of this type of crime, you could be placed on what criminals call a "sucker" list. These names are shared with other criminals, and you may be targeted in the future. Be aware of the possibilities of additional scam artists contacting you. DO NOT LET THIS WARNING KEEP YOU FROM FILING A CLAIM.

Unfortunately, the many successful stories of love found online make it even easier for scam artists, and scams are not just happening in the United States. "Last year in the UK, there were almost 4000 victims (http://www.bbc.com/news/uk-38678089) of romance fraud scammed out of $54 million. In Canada last year 750 victims lost $17 million (http://www.rcmp-grc.gc.ca/en/news/2017/13/victms-lose-14-million-romance-scams-2016)."[22]

If you have sent money to a pursuer or feel you are being scammed, contact your local police. In addition, the following fraud centers are available for you to contact immediately:

- **US**: FBI's Internet Crime Complaint Center (http://www.ic3.gov/)
- **Canada**: Canadian Anti-Fraud Center (http://www. antifraudcentre-centreantifraude.ca/index-eng.htm)
- **UK**: Action Fraud (https://www.actionfraud.police.uk/)

## Education and Purpose

Many successful couples have found love and a companion with online dating services. The story of my journey is not intended to discourage any one from using the services available for online dating. I share my experience for two major reasons: education and self-awareness.

**Education**: The tools I have provided to prepare singles for online dating will assist you selecting the safest online services available, along with detecting warning signs to watch for when online dating. With this information, I believe we can reduce the number of successful scams and the millions of dollars lost to victims each year across our nation and our world. Educate yourself on how to avoid this misfortune by learning all you can about the profile the individual has posted. Know the warning signs of a possible scam if you are in the midst of dating with an online dating service. *Take Your Time. Move Slowly.*

**Self-Awareness**: Being self-aware is the best tool for protecting yourself. Your purpose in life can seem very elusive but some unique purpose lies within each of us. Too often, we search everywhere but within our own soul. When your heart is lonely and you're functioning in life without purpose, you can become especially vulnerable to a scam artist. Educating yourself and focusing on your purpose in life can be the best tools for protecting yourself from fraud of any kind.

# Conclusion

As a professional woman, I did not feel proud of falling prey to a con artist. In fact, I felt ashamed and hid seven years of my life behind the reality of a story that I've now shared with you in this book. The weight of my own tragic experience, which I carried in my heart for too long, consumed my life for years. During my recovery after the scam, I grew spiritually—so much so that it became apparent to me that my search for many years was actually the search to "love myself." A lifetime of not loving myself? I could hardly believe it. But learning that I did not love myself for so many years—in fact, all my life—helped me see why I made the decisions I made that led to the paths I took and the circumstances that led to me becoming the victim (now survivor) of massive financial fraud.

Childhood and early adult years are formative years. At the time I was scammed, I had not overcome the pain points I had experienced in my lifetime. Searching for happiness often seems like a futile search, but I've learned that happiness is within ourselves, if we only take a moment and recognize its presence. As I traveled through this devastating episode of my life, I learned who I am and where I'm going. I have climbed huge mountains and struggled mightily, but I've also surfaced from dark waters. As I write now, my life is full of excitement, joy, and volumes of gratitude to those who have stood by me, quietly supporting me and this dark secret I had buried for years.

Catherine Ponder writes in her book, *The Dynamic Laws of Prosperity*, "Forgiveness is the Foundation of Healing."[23] I knew that if I was ever to move forward, I had to forgive the criminals who stole my money and, for a time, my life. Erasing anger from my heart for one of those criminals in particular was a major step in my healing process, which also included being able to forgive him. To allow myself this freedom, I wrote a letter of forgiveness to this man and lit a flame to it, finalizing the total experience.

After eighty-plus years of life, I have faced many challenges, but I have also learned that forgiving in the most difficult situations and being vulnerable—more naked than a newborn—is finding and living life in its true essence. Once I was able to forgive within my heart, the healing process for my body, mind, and spirit became part of my life.

o   o   o

The FBI estimates that approximately "fifteen percent of online dating scams go unreported."[24] I reported my own victimization to the police and the FBI very soon after it occurred. The rest of the story, however, remained in my heart, buried deep for many years. Very few people in my life knew it even occurred. In other words, what I didn't report to anyone was the humiliation and shame such a crime brings to victims like me. With this story of my journey, along with my best advice to assist you in finding love and companionship, I hope that you can stay true to yourself and not only report a crime of fraud to the police, but also share your experience with supportive people in your life. In addition to helping others, these actions can help dissipate the shame and humiliation you carry in your heart so that your soul can heal.

Along the way to my recovery, I studied many metaphysical subjects, such as psychic development and multi-dimensional awareness. Apollo, one of the psychics I studied with, assisted me in discovering my Divine Self. He has traveled the country as an award-winning motivational speaker, teaching classes on a vast array of metaphysical subjects. I carry one of his pieces of advice with me at all times. "Stuff happens," he says. "It's how you react that matters."[25] Taking charge of your actions and sharing what happened with other people who love you can start your own recovery process.

Mike Dooley's book, *Infinite Possibilities: The Art of Living Your Dreams*, stays on my reading table within easy reach. Attending his workshops, as well as joining one of his world cruises, has given me inspiration and tools for guidance. To deal with the monstrous emotional and financial losses that happened to me, I found strength and wisdom in these words of Dooley: "Whenever something unexpected or unthought of falls onto our path, it's always a stepping stone in a journey to a 'place' that we have been thinking about."[26] Dooley reaffirmed for me what God has always intended for each of us. We just don't always listen to God's messages and are often impatient.

This has been a journey of hard work. Through my determination to maintain a positive outlook, I have been able to overcome huge obstacles while staying focused on my end goals. I have realized many of my dreams, and I know there are more on the way. I now love myself, have found love with a new, wonderful companion, and openly reveal my love to help others experience the power of love.

### It's Love
*by Carole Kathryn*

*It's Love*
That clears my shame and doubt away,
And brings the smile back to stay.

*It's Love*
That heals the hurt and pain.
All now reveals it was not in vain.

*It's Love*
That creates memories not to forget.
While creating new with every step.

*It's Love*
That opens doors that once were sealed.
Love fills my heart.
At last it's healed.

# Suggested Reading

Brady, Lindsay, A., *As the Pendulum Swings: If It Isn't Hypnosis, Then What Is It?*, Oregon: Robert D. Reed Publishers, 2010.

Dooley, Mike, *Infinite Possibilities: The Art of Living Your Dreams*, New York: Beyond Words Publishing, Inc., 2009.

Dooley, Mike, *Manifesting Change: It Couldn't Be Easier*, New York: Simon & Schuster, 2010.

Dooley, Mike, *Leveraging the Universe*, New York: Beyond Words Publishing, Inc., 2011., New York: Atria Books, 2011, New York: A Division of Simon & Schuster, Inc. 2011.

Kornfield, Jack, *The Wise Heart: A Guide to the Universal Teachings of Buddhist Psychology*, New York: Bantam Books, 2009.

Ortner, Nick, *The Tapping Solution: A Revolutionary System for Stress-Free Living*, Carlsbad: Hay House, Inc., 2013.

Ponder, Catherine, *The Dynamic Laws of Prosperity*, USA: Spastic Cat Press, 2011.

Silverstein, Judith, MD, Lasky, Michael, JD, *Online Dating for Dummies*, New York: Wiley Publishing, Inc., 2004.

Tolle, Eckhart, *A New Earth Awakening to Your Life's Purpose*, New York: Plume, 2006.

Website, "Dating Site Reviews," https://www.datingsitesreviews.com/

# Acknowledgments

Without the support, love, and belief in me from the following people, this book would not have been possible. In the beginning, writing a book seemed to me to be an unbelievable accomplishment. Many have stood by me with encouragement to share my story.

I first want to thank Dr. Laura Bush, founder and CEO of Peacock Proud Press. You were a beacon of light for me from the first moment I stood in your workshop and told my story for the first time. You received my words of confession, buried deep in my heart, with love and respect. Your mentoring helped me articulate my thoughts about this long-held secret. Throughout this process, you continually encouraged me. Without your steadfast belief in my accomplishment during these tedious months of writing and sharing, I would not have completed this book. Your insight into my frustrations kept me on track. I extremely appreciate your personal concern and support for my long hours of work on this book. Thank you to your entire team. They always met their deadlines and gave me back exceptional work.

To Jane M. Powers, author, international speaker, entrepreneur, and coach, thank you for giving me the courage and the support necessary so that I could step on stage and tell my story. Your encouragement and teachings have prepared me to help others who are seeking love or who have been scammed. Working with you has filled me with boundless energy to embark on this last leg of my journey.

To Steven D. Keist, my lawyer, thank you for your nonjudgmental manner, ever-present since the first day I met you. You were always there for me during this long legal battle. You gave me the strength to persevere throughout this horrendous case. Thank you for always being readily available to offer me professional guidance, support, and friendship.

To the legal team, Craig Torbenson, the federal postal inspector; Paul

Rubin, the private investigator; and Debra and Denise, the special agents of the California Department of Justice. I offer each of you my respect and gratitude. You all worked relentlessly to uncover the fraud and reach closure. I am grateful for your professional, nonstop search for clues and for keeping in touch with me during the three years of this investigation and trial.

To my dear friend, Jean Ward, I am in deep gratitude to you. You always took the time to listen in my darkest hours, move me from tears to laughter, and encourage me to see the sunshine. Thank you for always being there to pick me up and for encouraging me to keep moving forward. Thank you for supporting me in writing this book and for always being there to listen while I shared my thoughts.

To Mychael James, ballroom owner and professional instructor, you have been my friend for many years. Dancing and music were part of my healing. Thank you for your support and encouragement as I wrote my story. It would have been a darker, lonelier journey without you.

To Lowell, one of my ballroom teachers, thank you for the keen insight into my struggle to keep a smile. You helped me rebuild my self-esteem and confidence, so I could perform in my winter years.

To Vikki Liles, a lawyer and dancer in my ballroom world, thank you for leading me to key professionals I needed in a dark moment, all while keeping my story in your confidence.

To all my other fellow dancers, many who were not aware of my situation, I offer my sincere gratitude. You were always there to share the joy of music, laughter, and dance.

To my friends, Judy A., who was there at my moment of need to file the report, Nancy S., who was always my long-distance confidante, and Zakea, who offered support through the years along many different avenues.

To my coworkers, Brooke, Judy, and Cheryl, for your quiet emotional support. You never questioned why I needed it. I very much appreciate our friendship.

To Lindsay A. Brady, C. Ht., your guidance in the study of hypnotherapy helped me move forward in my recovery. I will be forever grateful to the following leaders of the New Age movement, who have made their work available through books, live webinars, and workshops: Mike Dooley, Andy Dooley, Apollo, Deepak Chopra, Lorna Byrne, Eckhart Tolle, Gary Zukav, and Nick Ortner. Your willingness to share your wisdom with the world has inspired me in my recovery.

With all of this support, I am now ready to coach and guide others. For that, I am forever grateful.

# About the Author

Carole K. Zingula is a native of Iowa who currently resides in Arizona. She retired as a Registered Nurse after a twenty-five-career. As an accomplished speaker, seminar host, and educator, she delivered quality education and hope to professionals and the public regarding cancer. For that service, the American Cancer Society honored her as a "Nurse of Hope."

Carole's work ethic, creativity, and desire to help others led to additional ventures after retirement. She became an entrepreneur, owning and operating a floral business. Her passion for ballroom dance led to assisting in design and sales management for ballroom gowns and attire. Currently, Carole works as a licensed health insurance benefits advisor.

In her spare time, Carole ballroom dances, cares for her flowers, and visits family, including three children, seven grandchildren, and three great grandchildren who live in various parts of the country.

Carole's first-hand experience of financial loss, humiliation, and recovery from online dating fraud gives her valuable experience, knowledge, and tools to help others. She regularly speaks about why and how fraud can happen to anyone—and how to prevent it.

# Notes

1  "FBI Cautions Public to be Wary of Online Romance Scams," FBI Washington Public Information Office, February 7, 2018, https://www.fbi.gov/news/stories/romance-scams.

2  Lindsay A. Brady, *As the Pendulum Swings: If It Isn't Hypnosis, Then What is It?* (Oregon: Robert D. Reed Publishers, 2010), 378.

3  Harvey Waiver Law and Legal Definition, https://definitions.uslegal.com/h/harvey-waiver, 1979.

4  Mike Dooley, "Notes from The Universe," httsp://www.tut.com.

5  Sri Chinmoy, "Peace Begins When Expectation Ends," https://www.srichinmoycentre.org/sri_chinmoy/quotes.

6  Gary Zukav, *Spiritual Partnership: The Journey to Authentic Power* (New York: HarperCollins Publishers, 2010), 196-197.

7  "FBI Cautions Public to be Wary of Online Romance Scams," FBI Washington Public Information Office, February 7, 2018, https://www.fbi.gov/news/stories/romance-scams.

8  Sri Chinmoy, "Peace Begins When Expectation Ends," https://www.srichinmoycentre.org/sri_chinmoy/quotes.

9  Eckhart Tolle, *A New Earth Awakening to Your Life's Purpose* (New York: Plume, 2005), 181.

10 Brian Hay, "Romance Scammer Stories," https://www.aarp.org/money/scams-fraud/info-2015/online-dating scams.

11 Sri Chinmoy, "Peace Begins When Expectation Ends," https://www.srichinmoycentre.org/sri_shinmoy-quotes.

12 Barbara Sluppick, "Romance Scammer Stories, Are You Real?" https:www.aarp.org/money/scams-fraud/info-2015/online-dating scams.

13 Monica Whitty and Adam Johnson, *Truth, Lies and Trust on the Internet* (New York: Routledge, 2008), AARP The Magazine, https://www.aarp.org/money/scams-fraud-info-2015 online-dating.

14 Marisa Meltzer, "Avoid a Romance Scam When Using Dating Sites," https://www.consumerreports.org/dating-relationships/online-dating, Updated February 9, 2018.

15 AP Images for AARP Media, "Romance Scammer Stories," https://www. aarp.org/money/scams-fraud/info-2015.

16 AP Images for AARP Media, "Romance Scammer Stories," https://www. aaarp.org/money/scams-fraud-info-2015.

17 Doug Shadel and David Dudley, "Are You Real? Romance Scammer Stories," *AARP The Magazine*, https://www.arp.org/money/scams-fraud-info-2015 online-dating.

18 Sophie, How to Spot a Romance Scammer, https://scamalytics.com/ author/admin/, April 21, 2016.

19 Online Dating Association, Online Dating/Get Safe Online, https:// www.getsafeonline.org/social-networking/online-dating, https://www. onlinedatingassociation.org/uk, updated November 01, 2018.

20 Online Dating Association, Online Dating/Get Safe Online, https:// www.getsafeonline.org/social-networking/online-dating, https://www. onlinedatingassociation.org/uk, updated November 01, 2018.

21 AARP DATING, relationships (/home-family/friends-family/) December 2012, https://www.howaboutwe.com

22 Aimee O'Driscoll, "Online Dating and Romance Scams: How to Spot and Avoid Them, "https://www.comparitech.com/author/aimee, December 21, 2017.

23 Catherine Ponder, *The Dynamic Laws of Prosperity* (Spastic Cat Press 2011), 188.

24 Christine Beining, FBI Houston, "Romance Scams," https://www.fbi.gov/ news/stories/romance-scams, February 13, 2017.

25 Apollo Master Psychic, httsp://apollostarnetwork.com.

26 Mike Dooley, *Infinite Possibilities: The Art of Living Your Dreams* (New York: Atria, 2009), 22.

www.ingramcontent.com/pod-product-compliance
Lightning Source LLC
Chambersburg PA
CBHW030259130626
46549CB00002B/606